THE HUNGER GAMES

Suzanne Collins

AUTHORED by S.R. Cedars
UPDATED AND REVISED by Elizabeth Weinbloom

COVER DESIGN by Table XI Partners LLC
COVER PHOTO by Olivia Verma and © 2005 GradeSaver, LLC

BOOK DESIGN by Table XI Partners LLC

Published by GradeSaver LLC, www.gradesaver.com

First published in the United States of America by GradeSaver LLC. 2012

ISBN 978-1-60259-276-6

Printed in the United States of America

For other products and additional information please visit http://www.gradesaver.com

Table of Contents

Table of Contents

Table of Contents

Biography of Collins, Suzanne (1962-)

Though she has a long career of writing for children's television, Suzanne Collins has seen her reputation blossom since she began to write young adult novels. She began with the New York Times bestselling five-part fantasy/war series, *The Underland Chronicles*. And of course, her most acclaimed and popular work to date has been *The Hunger Games* trilogy, which the *New York Times* noted "revealed [her] outsize imagination for suffering and brutality." In addition to winning her a slew of awards, the novels have made Mrs. Collins popular enough to be named one of Time Magazine's Top 100 people in 2010.

Mrs. Collins's television work has also been much acclaimed. Her work includes young adult programs such as *Clarissa Explains It All* and *The Mystery Files of Shelby Woo*. She has also written for pre-school viewers on programs like *Little Bear* and *Oswald*. She has worked for many networks, including Nickelodeon and WB.

Ms. Collins has studied at the Alabama School of Fine Arts and at New York University, where she was awarded an MFA in Dramatic Writing. She lives in Connecticut with her husband and two children.

About The Hunger Games

The Hunger Games is the first novel in a trilogy that also includes *Catching Fire* and *Mockingjay*. Together, they are known as the *Hunger Games Trilogy*. This first novel has been on the *New York Times* Best Seller list for more than sixty weeks, and was named a New York Times notable book of 2008. It has garnered praise from many other writers, including Stephen King and Stephanie Meyer.

The trilogy has been distinguished by its masterful pastiche of adolescent coming of age tale and bleak dystopia. The first installment was published by Scholastic Press in September of 2008. As the author has stated in several interviews, its influences are many. They include the story of Theseus and the Minotaur, the author's experience with a father in the military, and her perception that, when watching television, the images of reality television and war were intermingling in her mind.

The novel functions as a traditional story and as an exploration of adolescent identity. However, its real success lies in how it intermingles severe social critiques through these common themes. The idea of a country where severe class divisions and brutal injustice to its citizens is masked by vacuous entertainment resonates with our contemporary world, which gives the novel an edge that distinguishes it amongst the many other runaway YA successes. Through the use of a perceptive and intelligent narrator, the novel traces how these influences can shape a young person's mind, and how grotesque the effects can be.

The book is significantly more violent and extreme than many of its competitors in the young adult market. In addition to severe physical and emotional violence, its narrator is refreshingly honest with her reader about the effects of poverty and death. The central conceit – young children are forced to fight one another to the death for the entertainment of their parents – is explored freely in the writing, which helps to explain its wild popularity among adults as well as children.

In spring of 2011, filming started for an adaptation of *The Hunger Games*, to be released by Lions Gate Entertainment in 2012.

Character List

Katniss Everdeen

The 16 year old narrator and protagonist of the novel. Katniss is an outsider to her country of Panem. As a member of the poorest class in the poorest District (District 12), Katniss is forced to scrounge and hunt for her family's survival. She takes care of her younger sister Prim and her mother by hunting with Gale, her closest friend. She is a professional hunter with great survival skills, and her best weapon is her bow and arrow. In order to stay successful, Katniss has developed a tough stoic attitude to life, which comes in handy once she is chosen to compete as District 12 representative in the Hunger Games. Deep down, Katniss has a deep compassion for others, and thrives on taking care of the helpless. She learns more about this part of herself during the Games.

Primrose Everdeen

Katniss's younger sister, 12 years old. She goes by "Prim." Prim is much more innocent and child-like than Katniss, and not just because she lacks the hunting aptitude of her older sister. Katniss makes it her life's priority to protect Prim from the hardness of life, and Prim thus serves as a personification of Katniss's deferred innocence. Prim has a pet goat named Lady, and works sometimes to help their mother with her duties as a healer.

Katniss's Mother

Katniss's mother is never named in the novel, but she is an important part of Katniss's life. After her husband's death, the mother was paralyzed by her grief, so much so that she did not provide for her daughters. This helplessness is what caused Katniss to begin hunting and gathering to protect the family. The mother has since recovered and works as an apothecary (which in Panem means a non-traditional "healer"), but Katniss has never forgiven her for having disappeared as she did. The mother was from a middle-class family, and married beneath her station when she married Katniss's miner father.

Katniss's Father

Katniss's father is never named in the novel, nor is he seen in the narrative. He was a miner who was killed in a mining explosion before the narrative begins. He was a very close to Katniss, and his death devastated her. Following his death, Katniss adopted a stoic attitude to life so as to provide for her family. Her father was also a wonderful singer.

Gale Hawthorne

Katniss's best friend and hunting partner in District 12. He is two years older than her. His last name is not provided by this novel, but is mentioned in the rest of the trilogy. Gale is characterized by Katniss as an attractive boy, though she claims there is no romance between them. He is a skilled hunter and a positive presence in her life. He is as poor as Katniss (if not more so), and equally responsible for providing for his family as she is. His father was killed in the same mine explosion that killed her father. Gale calls Katniss "Catnip."

Peacekeepers

The police force of Panem. They illustrate the toughness of Capitol laws, though the reader never confronts them directly in this first volume of the trilogy.

Greasy Sae

An old woman who trades commodities at the Hob, the District 12 trading post.

Madge Undersee

The daughter of District 12's mayor. Madge is very kind to Katniss, and gives her the mockingjay pin before Katniss heads off to the Hunger Games.

Mayor Undersee

Madge's father, and a big fan of the strawberries that Katniss sells to him. He is the mayor of District 12. He reads the Treaty of Treason at the reaping day ceremony. Described as a "tall, balding man."

Effie Trinket

A Capitol-appointed escort for the Games. She bears great contempt for District 12, and wishes she could be appointed a better district, even though she balances that contempt with extreme peppiness.

Haymitch Abernathy

One of the two sole District 12 citizens to have won the Hunger Games, and the only one surviving. As such, he serves as a mentor to his district's tributes. He is a heavy drinker, which makes him seem a buffoon to most, but once Katniss and Peeta impress him, he proves himself a rather adept mentor through establishing their unified front strategy. Though Katniss professes to despise him, she realizes through the novel that they are very much alike in their craftiness and ability to suppress their emotions.

Peeta Mellark

The male tribute chosen to represent District 12 in the Hunger Games, and Katniss's closest companion during the event. The son of a baker, Peeta belongs to the merchant class of the district. Peeta is an extremely kind boy, and once gave Katniss bread when they were much younger, a moment that she considers crucial to her survival in the period after her father's death. He has been in love with Katniss since he first saw her on their first day of school.

Peeta's Father

A baker in District 12. Katniss learns late in the novel that he once loved her mother. He visits Katniss after she is named tribute, and promises to keep Prim fed.

Venia, Flavius, and Octavia

Katniss's prep team for the Games, responsible for making her presentable (hygiene, make-up, etc.). They are a flamboyant and vacuous bunch, and while not outwardly antagonistic, represent the superficial nature of the Games.

Cinna

Katniss's stylist for the Games. Gentle and kind, and, in the early stages, one of the few people she trusts on her team. He helps realize Haymitch's unified front strategy by dressing Katniss and Peeta similarly. He also devises the "fire" theme that distinguishes Katniss as "the girl who was on fire."

Portia

Peeta's stylist for the Games. She works in tandem with Cinna.

Red-headed Avox

A servant in the center where Katniss stays while preparing for the Games. Years before, Katniss saw the girl get captured by Capitol representatives. The girl's companion, a boy, was killed in the incident. Katniss's inaction in this incident is a great source of her guilt. An Avox is a criminal whose tongue is removed by the Capitol as punishment for a crime.

President Snow

The President of Panem. Though he seems genial enough, his anger towards Katniss at the end of the novel suggests an uglier side.

Gamemakers

The team of Capitol representatives responsible for designing the arena and manipulating it for entertainment effect. They are described as robed, privileged, and uninterested in the well-being of the tributes whose deaths they control.

Atala

The Capitol representative who manages the Training Center for the tributes, before they head off to the arena for the Games.

The Careers

Tributes from richer districts who have illegally trained in order to succeed in the Games. They willingly attend as competitors, and Katniss refers to them as "the

Capitol's lapdogs." They include Clove, Glimmer, and Cato.

Rue

A female tribute from District 11, the second poorest district in Panem. She is 12 years old and Katniss associates her with Prim. They form an alliance in the Games, and Katniss is emotionally affected by her death, which is a major turning point in the novel.

Caesar Flickerman

The interview host for Games-related broadcasts. He maintains an image of perpetual youth through plastic surgery. An extremely affable fellow, Katniss notes how he makes his interview hosts feel at ease, a great irony since his job is to celebrate the brutish nature of the Games.

Claudius Templesmith

The announcer for the Hunger Games, described by Katniss as "legendary." His voice announces information to the tributes as they play, as well as narrating for the television audiences.

Clove

A female Career tribute known for her proficiency with knives. She is killed by Thresh when about to murder Katniss.

"Foxface"

A female tribute who operates through tactical avoidance of conflict. Katniss notices her hiding and darting through the woods, and nicknames her Foxface both for her animalistic features and her ability to stay quiet.

Thresh

The male tribute from District 11. Rue's counterpart. An extremely large boy who hides in the grassy fields and poses great challenge to the Careers. He saves Katniss's life, and is killed by Cato.

Glimmer

A female Career tribute. She fetches the bow and arrow at the beginning of the Games, and Katniss takes it from her body after she is killed by the tracker jackers that Katniss unleashes on the Careers.

Cato

The most vicious of the Career tributes, Cato becomes one of Katniss's primary antagonists. He holds great contempt for her personally, and throughout the Games hunts her.

Wolf Creatures

A legion of *muttations* (Capitol-managed mutations) that are sent after Katniss, Peeta, and Cato in the last leg of the Games. They are created from the reanimated corpses of the dead tributes.

Major Themes

Evolving identity

One of the central narratives in the novel is Katniss's shifting identity. At the beginning of the story, she considers herself thoroughly a "girl from the Seam." She finds dignity in her poverty and her ability to survive it through her hunting and gathering skills. While friendly with several members of the merchant class, she identifies herself most strongly with Gale, also the child of a deceased poor miner. The stoic strength this identity has given her provides the philosophy she thinks will help her succeed in the Games.

However, through the adventure, Katniss is forced to question both her identity as a "girl from the Seam" and her stoic detachment. In terms of the former, her relationship with Peeta, a boy from the merchant class, and her attraction to the luxury of the Capitol make her question whether she might belong somewhere different. And as she grows more and more indignant as she observes the brutality of the Games, she is forced to make many ethical decisions. She ultimately shows that deep down, she is a caring and empathetic person who disdains causing suffering (even to the antagonistic Career tributes), as opposed to being only a stoic hunter. This theme is reflected in a running conflict of passion vs. reason.

The sustaining power of love

Love proves to be integral towards keeping Katniss alive. She survived the difficult times following her father's death because she had Prim to look after. Her love for her sister (and her mother, though less explicitly) is what helps her to stay strong as a provider for the family. Likewise, Peeta's act of kindness with the bread, which she credits as having given her strength in that period, was dictated by his love for her, though she didn't know that at the time.

Further, her growing love for Peeta in the arena continually helps her. The most obvious way is by encouraging Haymitch to send her sponsor gifts. Though she claims she expresses affection only for the sake of the gifts, it can easily be argued that her true feelings for him are what help her survive the final phases of the Games.

Class

Panem is a country built on extreme class divisions. The districts are kept from contacting one another, and each is forced into a particular industry, thus limiting the social mobility of those within the district. Class is a strong tool used by the Capitol to keep its citizens distant from one another, hence limiting the chances of another rebellion. The *tesserae* is a prime example of how class keeps the poor resentful of the rich.

Katniss, as the girl from the Seam in District 12, is the poorest of the poor. Though friendly with some in the merchant class, she exhibits various class resentments throughout the novel. She associates the Career tributes with their richer districts, and has trouble falling for Peeta partly because he knows the privilege of the merchant class, comparing him to Gale, who knows poverty.

Spectacle

The concept of "spectacle" is that the ruling class keeps its transgressions hidden by distracting the population through entertainments. In contemporary society, the argument would be that our surplus of vacuous television promotes a consumer culture that keeps the lower classes from identifying how terribly they are oppressed.

This is very much what the Hunger Games do for the population of Panem. The Games are not treated by the citizens as brutish punishment, but rather as popular entertainment. By distracting the population with the Games, the Capitol keeps them from confronting greater injustices and potentially rebelling a second time.

Katniss is very aware of the spectacle throughout the novel. She is constantly aware that to be a victor, she must give the audience entertainment value. Her pride is another reason she wants to control her image for the audience. The existence and awareness of the spectacle cause Katniss a lot of character conflict, particularly in terms of her affection for Peeta, which she justifies as being for the audience but which the reader can identify as true feelings.

However, this theme is somewhat undercut by District 12's awareness of the horror of the Games. Collins seems to be saying that there is a nobility to being truly poor that allows them to see truths the more comfortable cannot. But this diminishes the parallel to real-world spectacle keeping oppressed classes from awareness of their oppression.

Stoicism

Stoicism is an ancient philosophy of withholding emotion for the sake of inner strength. In Roman times, stoicism meant, in a larger sense, the willingness to lose everything.

One of Katniss's strengths is her stoicisim, which she describes as her "indifferent mask." Because of the pressure to provide for her family, she has learned to stay focused on survival at the expense of her emotions, so much so that she doesn't realize how deeply she feels for Gale. Through the novel, her stoic determination proves a great asset towards succeeding at the Games, but it also masks her deep empathetic feelings for other people. Part of her journey is learning to accept her emotional side in addition to her stoicism.

Rebellion/Revolution

Much of Panem's totalitarian and controlling structure is intended to keep the districts from uniting into a second rebellion. The Capitol has orchestrated a system to keep its population distracted and separated from one another.

Katniss's story is partially the story of her becoming a revolutionary. When first chosen as tribute, Katniss immediately begins to formulate a plan to win, considering her antagonists as the other tributes. This makes Peeta's kindness and Rue's similarities to Prim problematic, since they make it harder for her to consider them enemies. However, as the novel progresses, Katniss begins to realize her true enemy is not anyone in the arena but instead those who put them all there: the Capitol.

This novel is the first of a trilogy, and by the end of the first book, Katniss is firmly convinced that the true evil is the system. It is the first step of revolutionary zeal that will drive her to confront the powers that be.

Community

The Capitol keeps its population in line partially by keeping them separated. It uses class and spectacle and District separation to keep anyone from growing close to anyone else. Katniss brings this sense of isolation with her into the arena, believing that success will come from staying apart from the others and considering everyone around her as an enemy.

Part of her growth in the novel is the realization that people are stronger when they are together. First through her alliance with Rue and then with Peeta, Katniss finds she survives better when part of a team. Her empathy for others is connected to the recognition that people are connected by shared humanity. Some of the most emotional moments come from this sense of community, as when District 11 gifts Katniss bread for her affection towards Rue. Her growing sense of community helps Katniss identify the Capitol as her society's primary antagonist.

Glossary of Terms

Acrid

Having an irritatingly strong and unpleasant taste or smell

Aloof

Not friendly or forthcoming; cool and distant

Apothecary

A druggist or chemist; in Panem, a "healer."

Barbarism

Absence of culture and civilization.

Cannibalism

The practice of eating one's own kind (i.e. humans eating humans)

Catacombs

Either an underground cemetery, or an underground construction resembling such a cemetery

Cornucopia

A symbol of plenty consisting of a goat's horn overflowing with sustenance.

Decadent

Luxurious and self-indulgent

Feral

Wild, uncivilized

Festering

To become rotten and offensive to the senses

Forage

To search widely for food and provisions

Grandeur

Splendor and impressiveness

Groosling

A wild bird found in the arena.

Haggle

To bargain persistently, usually with a merchant

Hovercraft

A vehicle that travels over land or water on a cushion of air provided by a downward blast.

Indifferent

Having no particular interest or sympathy; unconcerned

Iodine

A chemical solution, used in this novel to treat unclean water

Pretense

A false display of feelings, attitudes or intentions

Sustenance

Food and drink as source of strength and nourishment

Tessera

A small tablet of wood or bone used as a token in ancient Greece and Rome; in Panem a token for food in exchange for additional Hunger Game entries

Short Summary

The Hunger Games details the adventure of Katniss Everdeen, who is forced to engage in a fight-to-the-death tournament against other children. The novel takes place in Panem, a dystopic country built on what was once North America. In a world of limited resources, the despotic government run by the Capitol keeps its citizens in line by separating them into Districts and reinforcing severe class separations. But their strongest tool to promote disunion and to discourage rebellion is the Hunger Games: a yearly event where two tributes from each district are pitted against each other for the country to watch on television.

Katniss lives with her mother and younger sister Prim in District 12, the poorest of the districts. Ever since her father's death, she has been the family provider, hunting illegally in the woods outside the district with her friend Gale. The novel begins on the day of the "reaping," when each District must select two tributes, one male and one female, to represent them in the Hunger Games. When Prim is selected as the female tribute, Katniss offers herself as volunteer and is allowed to serve as tribute alongside Peeta, a middle class boy from the district.

The remainder of Part One of the novel follows the children as they are both trained for the brutal games and groomed to portray a certain image for the audience. She forces herself into a stoic determination to win, a philosophy made difficult by the kindly Peeta. The relationship is made even more fraught when Peeta confesses during a live interview that he has a crush on Katniss. Though she fears making emotional connections that could compromise her desire to win, she agrees to portray the image of a unified front, an idea proposed by their sponsor Haymitch.

The Games are held in an arena in a forested area. When they begin, Katniss rushes away from the excitement of the initial bloodbath and uses her hunting/survival skills to develop a strategy. She sleeps in trees and hunts game. Each night, faces of the dead are broadcast into the sky. As she stays hidden, she learns that Peeta has allied himself with the "Career Tributes," those tributes from the richer districts who train their entire lives for the Games.

Meanwhile, the Gamemakers, those who design the Games, continue to manipulate the surroundings in order to keep the Games entertaining. After a severe burn following a firestorm, Katniss is trapped in a tree above the Careers. That night, she makes contact with Rue, the youngest tribute, who Katniss associates with Prim. Rue is up a nearby tree and suggests she defeat the Careers by dropping a wasp nest on them. She does so, in the process getting stung herself but also scattering the Careers and gaining for herself a bow, her strongest weapon. The wasp stings produce hallucinations, which slow her down and almost cost her her life, until Peeta helps her to escape. She is understandably confused.

Katniss and Rue form an alliance and make a plan to destroy the supplies that are keeping the Careers powerful. Rue sets fires to distract them while Katniss pieces together that they are protecting their supplies with landmines reappropriated from a Gamemaker design. When she uses the mines to explode the supplies, she is blown backwards and knocked out of commission for a few days. She returns just in time to see Rue killed by another tribute, who then quickly becomes Katniss's first kill. As a small act of rebellion against the Capitol, which expects the tributes to dehumanize one another, Katniss sings to Rue and decorates her corpse with flowers before the body is fetched by the Capitol.

The Gamemakers announce that the rules have changed, and that the two tributes from a district can serve as co-victors. She then finds Peeta, who was cut badly after helping Katniss escape the Careers. She does her best to help him recover, but it isn't until Haymitch sends her a gift following a kiss she shares with him that she understands that playing up the romance angle could pay off.

They spend days growing closer in a cave, but Katniss lacks the skill to cure Peeta's wound. When the Gamemakers announce that a "feast" will be held to draw the tributes together for crucial supplies, she tricks Peeta and heads to the feast. In trying to get her gift, which she assumes is anti-infection medicine for Peeta, she is almost killed by a Career, but saved by the other tribute from Rue's district. Having heard of Katniss's kindness towards Rue, the tribute lets her live.

The medicine cures Peeta, and they spend more time growing closer in the cave. Once the Gamemakers dry up their water supplies, they prepare themselves and head out to face Cato, the only other surviving tribute. But their main challenge turns out not to be Cato, but several wolf-man creatures unleashed by the Gamemakers, creatures reanimated from the corpses of dead tributes. Katniss and Peeta escape by climbing to higher ground, while the other tribute falls and is tortured by the creatures. Finally, Katniss kills the tribute with her arrow out of mercy.

They have won the Games, but the Gamemakers rescind the rule about dual victors. Peeta and Katniss threaten to commit dual suicide, which would ruin the Games, and they are hence awarded a dual victory.

They are fetched by the Capitol representatives, and separated for a long period of recovery. When they are brought out to the audience again, Haymitch warns Katniss that she needs to overplay the lovers angle as a defense for her threat to commit suicide, which the Capitol considers an act of rebellion. Over the period of fanfare that follows, she takes his advice, which makes Peeta, who actually does love her, very happy.

When all is done, they head back to District 12, and Katniss lets slip along the way that her affection was always for the cameras. Though not the entire truth, she is torn between her old identity as a poor hunter, and the more complex one she shaped through the Games. Peeta is heartbroken, but understands they must maintain an image as they prepare to present themselves to their district.

Quotes and Analysis

"When I was younger, I scared my mother to death, the things I would blurt out about District 12, about the people who rule our country, Panem, from the far-off city called the Capitol. Eventually I understood this would only lead us to more trouble. So I learned to hold my tongue and to turn my features into an indifferent mask so that no one could ever read my thoughts."

Page 6, Chapter 1

This passage describes a few of Katniss's characteristics that are central to her journey through the novel. First, they illustrate that she has an inherent understanding of the injustices perpetuated by the Capitol, as well as an inherent revolutionary spark. However, she has learned in her life that prudence suggests a stoical outlook, which she adopts in order to not draw attention to herself. Her "indifferent mask" helps her to provide for her family. This forced attitude is one that she will challenge throughout the adventure in order to rediscover who she is deep down: a revolutionary with a deep sense of empathy for those plagued by injustice.

"As long as you can find yourself, you'll never starve."

Page 52, Chapter 4

This phrase is spoken by Katniss's father to her in one of her flashbacks. Literally, it was spoken when he introduced her to the plant katniss, an edible root and her namesake. However, it figuratively serves as a philosophy that will provide the key to Katniss's success. Her journey is one of discovering her true identity, which involves a balance between her stoic determination and her more emotional side. It is also telling that her father, the man whose death led her to eschew her emotional side, speaks this line.

"I'm ashamed I never tried to help her in the woods. That I let the Capitol kill the boy and mutilate her without lifting a finger. Just like I was watching the Games."

Page 85, Chapter 6

These are Katniss's thoughts about the redheaded Avox who serves her in her Capitol lodgings. The memory of her inaction continues to haunt Katniss, providing a challenge to her stoic demeanor. Deep down, she simultaneously knows that inaction was the prudent move to protect herself, and yet feels that she observed an injustice that she could have challenged. It reflects the deep division in her identity between reason and passion, and what's more, in this thought, she begins to compare inaction to that of the population who refuses to fight against the barbarous Games. This guilt is one of the first steps that leads Katniss towards establishing her revolutionary zeal.

"Gale gave me a sense of security I'd lacked since my father's death. His companionship replaced the long solitary hours in the woods. I became a much better hunter when I didn't have to look over my shoulder constantly, when someone was watching my back...Being out in the woods with Gale...sometimes I was actually happy."

Page 113, Chapter 8

On a literal level, this passage details how Gale became important to Katniss as a teammate. But it also illustrates that, deep down, Katniss possesses a self-knowledge that she never realizes until going through the Games. Much of her journey in the novel is learning to trust her feelings of community, to recognize that people are stronger when they work together. Her life as hunter taught her that stoic detachment was her most valuable asset, and she tries to use this in the arena. In spite of herself, she ends up allying with Rue and then Peeta, and these alliances strengthen her chances. By the end of the novel, she has come to realize the importance of trusting others, but this is not something she learns out in the arena, but rather something she knew deep down all along, as this quote illustrates.

"Why don't you just be yourself? ... No one can help but admire your spirit."

Page 121, Chapter 9

These quotes are spoken by Cinna to give Katniss guidance on how to best sell herself to the audience in her first interview with Ceaser Flickerman. The whole situation, as well as the work Haymitch does to help Katniss shape an image, speaks to the pervasiveness of the spectacle that is the Hunger Games. It is telling that Cinna's suggestion – that Katniss should just be herself – is almost revolutionary in a world where the spectacle is so highly prized. What's more, behind Cinna's suggestion is the message that everything Katniss needs not only to win the Hunger Games but also to become a hero is already inside of her. Her victory comes not from the stoic determination that makes her a good hunter, but moreso from her acceptance of her emotional and empathetic side. The revolutionary she approaches becoming by the end of the novel is someone she already is – she just has to learn to be herself and thereby accept it.

"They do surgery in the Capitol, to make people appear younger and thinner. In District 12, looking old is something of an achievement since so many people die early. You see an elderly person, you want to congratulate them on their longevity, ask the secret of survival. A plump person is envied because they aren't scraping by like the majority of us. But [in the Capitol] it is different. Wrinkles aren't desirable. A round belly isn't a sign of success."

Pages 124-125, Chapter 9

These are Katniss's thoughts after observing up close how youthful Caesar Flickerman continues to look because of plastic surgery. These thoughts emphasize how significantly class differences affect every element of a person's life and perspective in Panem. Katniss confronts her contradictory feelings about class through her early stages of being a tribute, as she is overwhelmed by the luxuriousness of the Capitol. And yet she considers herself simply a "girl from the Seam." Class resentments play a recurring role in the novel and the arena, and the pressures of poverty actually provide her with a strength and resilience that helps her succeed.

"I bite my lip, feeling inferior. While I've been ruminating on the availability of trees, Peeta has been struggling with how to maintain his identity. His purity of self."

Page 142, Chapter 10

Katniss thinks this after Peeta confesses to her on the roof that what he wants most in the Games is to not compromise himself. His confession forces her to directly confront a contradiction within herself: while she has chosen to maintain a stoic determination for victory, she actually has strong empathetic feelings for other people, motivated partly by hatred of the Capitol. When Peeta expresses how firmly he is to his own identity, it cuts Katniss to the quick. She knows deep down that she is a bigger person than the hunter obsessed with victory. Her journey through the novel is to accept her human, caring, loving characteristics.

"As I hike along, I feel certain I'm still holding the screen in the Capitol, so I'm careful to continue to hide my emotions. But what a good time Claudius Templesmith must be having with his guest commentators, dissecting Peeta's behavior, my reaction. What to make of it all? Has Peeta revealed his true colors? How does this affect the betting odds? Will we lose sponsors? Do we even have sponsors? Yes, I feel certain we do, or did."

Page 165, Chapter 12

These thoughts, which take place during the period when Katniss believes Peeta is working with the Careers, show how she aims to operate while in the arena. She consciously chooses to play to the spectacle, maintaining her stoic demeanor not only for success but to attract sponsors. There are countless other examples of this throughout the novel. Though it's clear to the reader in this passage that she feels betrayed by Peeta's seeming alliance, she won't admit that to herself. Instead, she denies her emotions and focuses only on how the betrayal tactically affects her chances. This is not truly who she is deep down, and her time in the arena will help her discover that.

"Rue's death has forced me to confront my own fury against the cruelty, the injustice they inflict upon us. But here, even more strongly than at home, I feel my impotence. There's no way to take revenge on the Capitol. Is there?"

Page 236, Chapter 18

This passage shows Katniss's wakening consciousness to the pervasiveness of the injustice perpetuated by the Capitol. Katniss is beginning to lose her stoic detachment and identify her true antagonist as the Capitol. She has not yet recognized that the answer to victory will lie in trusting her community. However, the indignation that drives her revolutionary zeal is beginning to manifest in this passage. The first step towards discovering her true identity will involve her more fully accepting her emotional side, something that begins to happen after Rue's death.

"The idea of actually losing Peeta hit me again and I realized how much I don't want him to die. And it's not about the sponsors. And it's not about what will happen back home. And it's not just that I don't want to be alone. It's him. I do not want to lose the boy with the bread."

Page 297, Chapter 22

One of Katniss's most extreme emotional conflicts is how to understand the burgeoning relationship between her and Peeta in the arena. Because of the spectacle, she is able to convince herself that it's all a show to play to Haymitch's unified front strategy. But there's plenty of dramatic irony in the reader's awareness that she is falling for him. What's more, in calling him "the boy with the bread," she connects him to the kindness he performed for her so long before. Such selfless kindness is a virtue she herself possesses, though she considers it a weakness until she learns to accept it. This passage, unusually forthright for Katniss, is a moment where she admits to herself the depth of the feelings that helped her win. Through most of the preceding adventure, she is much less self-aware of her feelings.

Summary and Analysis of Chapter 1

CHAPTER ONE (START OF PART ONE)

The narrator and protagonist of *The Hunger Games*, a 16 year old girl named Katniss Everdeen, wakes up to find her little sister Prim has left the bed they share and curled up next to their mother. Katniss understands – it is the "day of the reaping," the first stage of the horrific Hunger Games that she will explain to the reader over the first few chapters.

Instead of waking her family, Katniss heads out to hunt, introducing her reader to her surroundings as she does. Katniss lives in a dystopic society built on the ruins of what was once North America, now named Panem. Panem is currently separated into 12 districts, each of which serves a specific purpose for the society, and is ruled from the distant sparkling Capitol. The Capitol heads a totalitarian government that controls its population primarily through the yearly ritual of the Hunger Games. Though the full details of the society are not revealed until later in the chapter, it's useful to understand them. After North America was destroyed through myriad disasters, Panem was founded by the Capitol. Seventy-five years earlier, the Capitol's control was contested by the districts, which rebelled. In what is now termed the "Dark Days," the twelve districts were defeated and a thirteenth district was obliterated as warning against further rebellion.

The Capitol has an even more devious structure to keep its citizens in line, though: the Hunger Games. Every year, each district must supply, through a lottery process, two "tributes" (both aged 12 to 18, one male, one female), who are forced to fight to the death in a large outdoor arena until one victor remains. The expectation is that the Hunger Games be treated as a spectacle, a great source of entertainment that all citizens are obliged to follow as audience. The Games illustrate how thoroughly Panem citizens are at the mercy of the Capitol, since it keeps them subdued by making them complicit in the atrocities as audience.

Since the rebellion, society has significantly stratified, particularly in terms of economic and social caste. Not only is the coal-mining District 12 on the lowest rung of social standing, but Katniss lives alongside her mother and sister in the poorest area of District 12, nicknamed "The Seam." On the edge of the Seam lies a large field called the Meadow, past which stands a fence that separates the population from the unsettled woods. The woods are dangerous due to wild animals, and illegal to explore or hunt in. Stealing and hunting are both punishable by death, if the perpetrator is caught by the Peacekeepers, or federal police.

But that's no concern for Katniss, who supports her family through hunting game and gathering roots in the woods. She learned these trades from her father, a man she loved dearly but who was killed in a mine explosion five years before the novel starts. When the shock of the tragedy left her mother near-catatonic and useless,

Katniss had no choice but to turn to this illegal trade to support her family, which she does not only through gathering food but also by trading her wares for other commodities in the Hob, an old warehouse that now serves as the district's black market. Her mother has recovered and continues to work as a healer, but Katniss has not quite forgiven her for having almost let her own daughters starve to death. Her mother's family had held some social standing as healers, but that was lost when her mother married her father, a common miner.

Katniss slides under the fence and heads out into the woods, fetching her hidden bow and arrow along the way. The weapon was crafted by her father and she has made herself a master at its use. She has become a consummate hunter with a trained stoicism. Where she once was happily critical of her society, she has learned not only to stay safely quiet but also to "turn [her] features into an indifferent mask." The only real joys she has are in protecting Prim and in hunting with her best friend, Gale.

On her excursion, she meets Gale, a boy about her age and her frequent hunting partner. He gifts her some fresh bread and they joke together. Her affection for him is unmistakable, though she insists there is nothing romantic between them. Enjoying their last moments before they must both report to the town square to find out who will be chosen as this year's tributes, Gale suggests they run away together. For Katniss, the idea is impossible since she must take care of Prim and, less obligingly, her own mother. Gale and Katniss fish together and gather some greens, which they then bring to the Hob. They trade there with Greasy Sae and others for some bread, salt, and paraffin.

There are some goods that they trade to particular customers, mainly in the merchant class of District 12. One of these is Mayor Undersee, who enjoys their strawberries. When they stop by his house to sell them, they are greeted by his daughter Madge. Though she is a nice girl, her privileges – exemplified in this moment by a small gold pendant she wears, which is very valuable – rub Gale the wrong way and he speaks rudely to her about her chances of being chosen as a tribute.

Katniss explains Gale's resentment. Each child, age 12 to 18, is required to enter his or her name for the district's lottery, with the older children putting their names in proportionally more times. However, Panem uses a system wherein children can enter their names extra times in exchange for *tesserae*, vouchers for a year's worth of meager grain and oil. Obviously, this system discriminates against poorer citizens who need the extra resources and hence make themselves more likely tributes. Both Katniss and Gale have had to enter their names multiple times from the time they were 12, whereas someone like Madge has always been able to enter the minimal number of times. Katniss reflects that this unfairness is not accidental, but yet another way that the Capitol encourages distrust amongst its citizens so as to limit the chances of unity within the districts.

Gale and Katniss separate the rest of their goods, and then Katniss heads home to prepare for the reaping. This is Prim's first reaping, and Katniss has refused to allow her to take out any tessarae, though Katniss's name is entered twenty times at this point. Still, as they prepare a stew and dress pretty for the reaping, Katniss is worried about her powerlessness. They drink some milk from Prim's pet goat, Lady, and then head to the square, where attendance is mandatory for all citizens.

Camera crews are perched everywhere, the first indication of the ubiquity of the televised spectacle of the Hunger Games. On a stage, Mayor Undersee and Effie Trinket, the Capitol representative for the district, begin the festivities. The Mayor tells the history of Panem and the Hunger Games, reads the Treaty of Treason (which ended the war), and then reads the list of past District 12 victors. In the 73 years of the Games, only two have won – and the only current survivor, Haymitch Abernathy, arrives on the stage as his name is read. He is a drunk, and is drunk enough now to stumble into the chairs. It's an embarrassing moment, especially because all of this is being recorded and televised throughout Panem.

Katniss is extremely nervous through the commotion, and seeks solace by looking across the square at Gale before hearing the worst possible news: when Effie Trinket reads the name of the female tribute, it is that of her sister, Primrose Everdeen.

ANALYSIS

Though it's easy to classify *The Hunger Games* as an adventure story, its implications are far deeper. Clear from the very beginning of the novel is the biting criticism of our society and economic divisions. But equally important is the complexity of the narrator's characterization, which will develop to sustain growth and increasing conflict over the course of the novel and two sequels as well.

Katniss's character conflicts are the most immediate, since she is the story's narrator. She narrates in the present tense, an effective choice since that leaves the reader uncertain whether she will survive the Games intact. Were the story narrated in past tense, it would indicate to us that she must have survived since she is telling the tale. The narration is also effective in providing dramatic irony throughout the novel, as we can infer much about Katniss both from what she chooses to tell us and how she chooses to tell it.

Katniss is an example of a stoic hero – she is well aware of the unfairness of the world around her, having had to grow up so quickly to provide for her mother and Prim. However, she has quashed both her emotional responses to her totalitarian society as well as her childish identity so that she can maintain the hardness necessary to be an effective hunter and provider. A contemporary definition of a stoic is one who does not show his or her emotions, but the tradition of stoicism, going back to the Greeks, is much deeper. In the classical philosophies, a stoic is one who steels himself to lose everything in order to find true freedom. Katniss will, through the novel, come to accept this philosophy while simultaneously realizing that she does have a deeply empathetic emotional side.

But in Chapter One, she has chosen to adopt an "indifferent mask" so as to avoid becoming the woman her mother became after her husband's death – an emotionally overcome person who was incapable of providing for her family. In fact, it seems that she has eschewed passion and tenderness ever since her father's demise. Katniss forces herself not to consider any romantic feelings for Gale, though the reader sees right away that this is somewhat disingenuous. She also has no playfulness in her life. As strong as she is, we should never forget that she is 16 years old. Instead of allowing herself the joys of childhood, she has transferred all hopes for childish innocence to her sister Prim, who serves as a personification of innocence for her. She not only refuses to allow Prim to hunt, but is also convinced she will spare her sister whatever hardships are possible. So while Prim gets to stay an innocent, Katniss has become an adult, trading in the Hob, acting as provider, and throwing away childish things. All of these elements are set up in Chapter 1 to be challenged throughout her adventure.

Katniss is the reader's way into the story, but the story has implications far greater than she could ever know. *The Hunger Games* can easily be viewed through a Marxist lens, since at its core is a vicious criticism of how class divisions are maintained not merely through the threat of punishment, but also through spectacle, used to divert the masses from confronting the true injustice in their world.

The social class divisions are extreme in Panem. Not only is the divide between the wealthy (who we don't see up close until the Capitol in Chapter 4) and the poor enormous, but it is openly acknowledged by the use of Districts. Gone is the "rugged individualism" that historically is associated with North America, where a citizen could work hard and do whatever he or she wants through intelligence, skill, and force of will. Instead, the Capitol has created a system where each district is forced to commit to one industry. It is not accident that the social mobility we associate with the United States has been traded for what resembles a medieval guild system, where children have no choice but to enter the occupation of their parents. What's more, the workers of each district are unable to reap the benefits of their work. This is apparent because District 12, which provides coal, an energy source, is nevertheless deprived of continual electricity. Materials are produced by a working class, but are then appropriated by a higher authority. Thus, there is no possibility that District 12 will ever grow more prosperous, even though it bears the acknowledged low spot on the social ladder.

Even within District 12, the class divisions are apparent – Katniss is the poorest of the poor, living in "the Seam." Some resentments surface through the chapter, especially when she and Gale confront the Mayor's daughter. And finally, the most severe indicator of class divisions in Panem is the use of *tesserae*, the system of trading extra entries in the lottery for food supplies. This system is a blatant "poor tax," ensuring that the poor can never crawl from their poverty and in fact punishing them for it. It calls to mind Harlem Renaissance writer James Baldwin's famous saying: "Anyone who has ever struggled with poverty knows how extremely expensive it is to be poor."

The severity of the injustice raises the question why the society does not revolt, especially since they are a population capable of revolution. They rebelled once and lost, but things seem to have only gotten worse. It is from this question that the novel's most extreme social statement becomes apparent, a statement that indicts not only the brutal Capitol for Panem's injustice, but in fact all of society itself. It is a great irony that Panem civilization is maintained through the use of such an uncivilized practice as the Hunger Games. Yet the Capitol is so proficient at shrouding the Games in ritual and tradition – see the ceremony of the reaping for myriad examples – that this brutality becomes the linking social force. The population, forced to watch these games, nevertheless revels in them to the point that they no longer question the brutality. Katniss, our hero, who otherwise is full of such deep love for her family and friend Gale, never seems to question the Games in this Chapter. The criticism in here derives from the theory of the "spectacle," the idea that the masses of our society are distracted by ubiquitous entertainment so that we do not realize the truly terrible injustices being perpetrated. In other words, though the poor in our world are a powerful force in numbers, they are kept from rebelling through a world built on commodities, on vacuous television entertainment, and on traditions that they do not question. This is very much the case in the Hunger Games, where the games have the air of an extremely popular reality television show. Collins suggests that we allow ourselves to be distracted by vacuous, uncivilized entertainments that only suggest the lower qualities of humanity, while the world is growing more unjust by the day, the wealth gap increases, atrocities are committed in the name of justice, and lies are spoon-fed to the population through these very entertainments. Our very fascination with the details of the Games - which Collins will voyeuristically describes for us through the remainder of the novels - is a reflection of our own willingness to allow ourselves to be enraptured by such spectacle.

Finally, it is worth considering the influence of Greek and Roman history and literature on the novel, all of which is set up in the first chapter.

The first is the connection between the Hunger Games and Roman gladiator fights. Though gladiator fights are often portrayed as heroic in our popular entertainments, the truth is they were horrific and violent events, where lower rungs of society were put in a ring to battle to the death while thousands of people watched complacently, unaware of the ironic separation between the great civilization of Rome and the uncivilized brutality they were sponsoring. The games in Rome grew progressively more frequent and violent with growing unemployment as the Roman empire expanded, bringing more slaves in for labor and hence taking jobs from citizens. In order to keep its ever-growing lower classes from revolt, Roman emperors sold the games as a great Roman tradition, in effect orchestrating a "spectacle" to keep people in line. Another Roman connection is in the tradition of the Stoic. Roman tragedian Seneca is connected with the school of stoicism, particularly the idea that by being willing to give up everything, one can find freedom and greatness. This concept, very much tied to Katniss, is a final connection to Rome. The end of the first chapter, when Katniss effectively gives her own life for Prim's, is the first step towards this form of stoic heroism. A character named Seneca also provides an important realization of her stoicism at the end of the novel.

Names are also carefully chosen for significance. The generic name for katniss the plant, for which Katniss Everdeen was named, is Sagittaria, from "sagitta," the Latin word for "arrow." Sagittarius is a Zodiac sign which is associated both with archery and with fire. In later chapters, fire will become Katniss's symbol in the Games. Panem is the name of the country in which the story takes place, and while the name evokes a corruption of Pan-American, "panem" is also the Latin for bread. This is a reference to the expression "panem et circenses," or "bread and circuses." In the waning days of the Roman empire, the increasingly stratified population was manipulated into submission through the provision of cheap food and distracting spectacle - much like the citizens of Panem. Finally, the "tesserae" of ancient Roman times was a token exchanged for grain, and was also used as a theater ticket and as dice.

Summary and Analysis of Chapters 2-4

CHAPTER TWO

As Katniss sees her sister moving in terror towards the stage, she leaps into the crowd and volunteers herself as replacement for Prim. While volunteers are rare, they are permitted, and so Katniss is ushered onstage, where she wonders whether the Mayor remembers the sad day long ago when he presented her with a medal to honor her father's demise. Gale steps forward to pull Prim away.

Though distraught, Katniss stoically keeps herself from crying, knowing that to do so would be to reveal weakness to the television viewers and, worse, to the foes she will face in the Hunger Games. Her awareness of the viewing population will be a recurring concern throughout her story.

Katniss is proud to see that none in the crowd applaud what has happened, and regard it as a small show of bravery against a Capitol that expects them to act as an excitable audience. What's more, they join together in a traditional gesture of support, by touching their fingers to their lips. She is almost brought to tears, but Haymitch's buffoonery keeps her solid when, on his way to congratulate her, he trips off the stage and is knocked unconscious.

As he is taken away, Effie reads the name of the male tribute: Peeta Mellark, the son of the baker. This name saddens Katniss, since Peeta once showed her a great act of kindness she has never forgotten. She explains how, in the period after her father's death when her mother was useless and she had not yet learned to hunt, she had been caught by Peeta's cruel mother while trying to steal some scraps from the baker's trash bin. She was standing out in the rain, still shocked from the reprimand, when she heard the mother curse and whip her son Peeta for burning two loafs of bread. When Peeta came out to throw the ruined bread away, he gave them to Kaniss instead, which not only fed her family for the day but also gave her a hope that sustained her for many years. When she saw him the next day at school, his eye blackened from his mother's beating, his presence led her to glance at a dandelion, which then reminded her that her father had taught her skills she could use to survive. Though they never spoke at school after that, Kaniss has harbored a belief that Peeta burnt the bread on purpose so he could give it to her, and remains thankful.

The thought of having to kill this boy to whom who she owes so much sickens her, and her only release is hoping one of the other twenty-two tributes will kill him first.

CHAPTER THREE

After the Panem anthem is played, the tributes are walked into the Justice Building and left in a room, which she calls the "richest place I've ever been" because of its luxury. She continues to battle her tears to maintain her image.

Her mother and sister are allowed to see her, and she quickly lectures them on all the responsibilities they must remember to fulfill so that they can not only survive but also prevent Prim from taking tessarae. She is particularly stern with her mother, demanding that the latter not fall back into the self-pity that had paralyzed her after her husband's death. Though she promises Prim she will win, Katniss is certain it's impossible, considering the bigger, well-nourished and better-trained kids from wealthier districts.

The Peacekeeper orders her family out and then admits Peeta's father, the baker. She knows him primarily through trade, and seems unsure why he's there. He gives her a bag with cookies, after which they sit in silence for a while. Before he is led out, he assures her he will keep Prim fed.

Next is another unexpected guest, Madge. She insists that Katniss wear the circular gold pin she noticed earlier – up close, Katniss can see it's a bird in flight (and the image from the book's front cover).

Finally comes Gale. She insists again that there is nothing romantic between them, but realizes how close he truly is to her. He reminds her to try and obtain or make her own bow if possible, and that she is a skilled hunter who knows how to kill, even if it's never been people.

Gale is forced to leave, and Katniss is brought by car (her first time in one!) to the train station, which is teaming with reporters. Her practiced stoicism helps her maintain a façade whereas Peeta's face is stained from tears. As travel is outlawed between districts, she has obviously never been on a train before either, and the new experience leads her to recall what she's learned about Panem's geography. She recalls that the Capitol was built in what was once the Rockies, and that District 12 sits in what was once Appalachia.

Her train compartment is yet another step up in luxury for her, with nice clothing and a hot shower easily accessible. She takes a closer look at the pin Madge gave her, and realizes the bird is a "mockingjay," a species of genetically altered bird that the Capitol had devised during the rebellion. Though bred to memorize and repeat human speech (so as to act as spies), the mutated birds proved ineffective and were let out to the wild, where they mated with common mockingbirds and maintained the ability to replicate human melodies. The image leads her to remember her father, who sung wonderfully and appreciated mockingjays.

Effie fetches Katniss to a succulent dinner with her and Peeta. She is shocked at having such a fine dinner, and the exquisite detail she uses to describe her meals becomes a repeated motif throughout the novel. When Effie expresses her pleasure at their use of utensils, lambasting previous District 12 tributes for their "savage" table manners, Katniss eats with her hands to express her disapproval of Effie's attitude.

She and Peeta are brought to watch the recap of the reapings throughout the districts, and they get their first glance at those who will be their opponents. Katniss is particularly affected to see a 12-year old from District 11, whose apparent frailty reminds her of Prim. After watching their own reaping repeated, Effie reminds the children that Haymitch's sobriety is of value to him, since, as their district sponsor, he is responsible for lining up sponsors who can pay to have gifts sent to them during the games, an important boon towards survival. Haymitch walks in at the end of this speech, so drunk that he vomits everywhere.

CHAPTER FOUR

Peeta offers to help Haymitch clean himself up. The offer makes Katniss grateful but also reminds her not to be too affected by his kindness since they will soon be opponents. She remembers again her early days of learning to hunt and provide for her family. One skill she mastered was identifying which herbs, roots and plants were safe to eat or use. She recalls how her father once introduced her to her namesake, the edible root Katniss, and how he told her "As long as you can find yourself, you'll never starve." Her memories make her feel guilty for having been too stern with her mother, and sad about home. She goes to bed without wearing any of the fancy clothes they've offered her. She knows her look will soon be out of her control, defined by an appointed Games stylist.

Effie wakes and then chaperones her to an overflowing breakfast. Watching the drunk Haymitch at breakfast, she realizes she detests him and wonders whether previous District 12 tributes lost partially because he was too much of a clown to line up decent sponsors. When Haymitch makes a joke mocking their plight, Peeta retorts sarcastically and Haymitch punches him. Katniss drives her knife into the table near his hand, and he realizes that he might actually have fighters this year. After verbally assessing their skill-sets, he agrees to stay sober enough to help them.

His first command comes as they arrive at the station. He makes them promise to acquiesce to the demands of their stylists, no matter what they think. Meanwhile, Katniss is overwhelmed by the grandeur of the Capitol, which is much more fantastic in sight than it ever was on TV. She is surprised to see Peeta playing to the gathered crowd, until he reminds her that by attracting fans, they attract sponsors and improve their chances at survival. She realizes again that she must stay wary, for "the boy who gave [her] the bread" is also playing a shrewd game that will ultimately mean he has to kill her.

ANALYSIS

Katniss's stoicism provides great benefit almost right away. Though undoubtedly overcome by emotion, she forces herself to focus immediately on the Games to come, by refusing to cry and hence confess a weakness that might hurt her later. The conflict of passion vs. reason (reflected in her stoicism) kicks into full force now that the story has begun.

Throughout these chapters, she exhibits a great command over her emotions. First, she continues to hold back her tears, in stark contrast to Peeta, whose eyes are red and swollen by the time he leaves the Justice Building. Even when her family visits her, Katniss refuses to let herself give in to emotion, instead lashing out a bit harshly at her mother, demanding the latter protect the family and not lapse back into the self-pity Katniss so disdains. The choice to rationally lecture her mother rather than emotionally comfort her will be one Katniss later questions.

This conflict between reason and passion establishes another deep theme, that of personal identity. This is most apparent in these chapters through her response to Peeta, which provides a stark contrast to her stoic demeanor. Peeta once showed Katniss a great kindness by giving her bread when she needed it, and her recollection of the event illustrates how deeply she was affected by it. But Katniss can only consciously confront these memories as a debt owed. The idea of an unconditional kindness is not only hard for her to comprehend, but she also feels that to think in such broad emotional terms about Peeta could prove a liability. After all, she has to kill him if she is to win the Games. She only confronts her feelings for and about Peeta in terms of their functional value, which shows that she is unable to fully accept her identity as a full, caring human being. She will battle with this as the adventure continues.

There are three additional elements that illustrate this conflict. The first is Gale's visit to her in the Justice Center. She is able to show much more emotion for him than even for her family, suggesting that he symbolizes a different world for her than they do. Where her family requires her to focus on order – survival, civilization, reputation, class – Gale is a symbol to her of a wild and unfettered humanity. Through him can she begin to approach her true nature as a child with deep, powerful emotions. The emotions are still muted in the scene with Gale, but they're there nonetheless. The second element is the introduction of Rue via the television replays of the various reapings. By immediately associating Rue with Prim, who the reader knows is the personification of Katniss's innocence, she is opening herself to a potential conflict that will later force her to question her identity as a stoic hunter. The third element is one of the novel's most enduring metaphors: the mockingjay pin. Though its significance will only be made clear later, it sets up both that Katniss associates music (which mockingjays repeat) with her father. Already, the sense is given that this mockingjay will serve as symbol for Katniss's emotional growth.

The mockingjay pin also will symbolize another arc of the novel: Katniss's revolutionary awakening. From Chapter 1, the reader sees that the entire society is complicit through its silence in the horrors perpetuated by the Capitol. The Capitol's system – the Hunger Games, perpetual poverty, etc. – are meant to separate people and discourage any further revolution. In these chapters, Katniss gets her first sense of how community can stand together when the crowd refuses to applaud her selection as tribute, and in fact shares a small rebellious act by indicating their support. This introduces two other themes, community and rebellion. So accustomed to relying solely on herself, Katniss will have to learn to work within a community, and her nascent rebellions against Effie and Haymitch show us that it's not going to be an easy transition for her.

Lastly, these chapters indicate that the deprivations of poverty make Katniss immediately susceptible to the charms that fortify the spectacle. Her passionate descriptions of the food she eats – all so luxurious for so poor a girl – begin in these chapters and will continue throughout. The delicious food and luxurious accommodations are like the carrot to keep her moving forward, unaware that by accepting these gifts, she plays into their hands. This also associates with the ongoing theme throughout the series of the power of gifts and debt, and who is willing to accept gifts from whom.

Summary and Analysis of Chapters 5-6

CHAPTER FIVE

Katniss is put through a rigorous grooming routine in the Remake Center, where she is scrubbed immaculate and her body rid of hair. Her prep teams includes Venia, Flavius, and Octavia, a flamboyant bunch who don't realize that their horror at the hygiene she's learned in District 12 is highly patronizing.

When they are done, she meets her main stylist, a young man named Cinna who she finds both endearing and attractive. He admires the simple braid that her mother tied for her, and surprises her by confesses he was not assigned the usually undesirable District 12, but in fact requested it. He brings her to a lunch, another fine meal available at moment's notice, and acknowledges that their luxury must seem despicable to her.

As tributes are usually dressed to indicate somehow the industry of their district, Katniss is afraid she'll be embarrassed as have previous District 12 tributes by unsightly coal themes. But Cinna's idea is to suggest coal through fire, and designs a fire-colored costume and cape that will actually be lit with synthetic flame during her introduction to the public. He daydreams of her being known as "the girl who was on fire."

When she and Peeta join again, to be introduced, she sees they are dressed in tandem. Cinna and Peeta's stylist, Portia, are working together. Despite her attempt to distance herself, she and Peeta laugh and comfort one another as they watch their soon-to-be opponents paraded out in pairs, district by district. As they are let out, now aflame, Haymitch instructs them to hold hands, which Katniss does before starting to, for the first time, play to the crowd herself.

Their chariot ride and its associated fanfare actually gets her excited, a mixed feeling because she will soon be asked to murder. They arrive at President Snow's mansion, and after he gives a speech, they are let in, where she notices the other tributes eye them angrily for the attention their flames received. Though she still doesn't trust Peeta, she recognizes the strategy of a unified front and pretends closeness.

CHAPTER SIX

They are introduced to the Training Center, where each pair and their team are assigned their own floor. Both Haymitch and Effie will live there as well. Their lodgings provide yet another step up in luxury. Katniss plays with all the gadgets in her room until Effie calls her to dinner. As they eat and begin to plan strategy, Haymitch shows a newfound lucidity. When Katniss recognizes one of their dinner servants, a red-headed girl, the adults are shocked and dismissive, since this girl is an *Avox*, a criminal whose tongue was cut out. It is a crime to speak to an Avox casually, so Peeta comes forward and lies to cover for Katniss's slip, suggesting the Avox just resembles someone from their school.

They all watch the replay of the ceremony, and Katniss begins to piece together Haymitch's strategy, realizing the unified front is a type of rebellion against the idea that every tribute works only for his or herself.

In the corridor, Peeta grills her about the girl, and Katniss is unsure whether to reveal her secret to him. Peeta suggests they check out the roof, presumably where their conversations cannot be monitored. Outside, Katniss admires the sight of so much electricity and looks down at the excitable streets of the big city. Near a garden, where fans will block out any eavesdropping devices, Katniss tells him how one day, she and Gale were out hunting and saw this girl and another boy in tattered clothes, fleeing through the woods. She didn't try to help them, but instead spied from the brush as a hovercraft appeared above, capturing the girl in the net and murdering the boy by spear. The girl and Katniss made eye contact as the former was pulled up into the hovercraft, and Katniss continues to feel guilt over her inaction. Peeta offers her his jacket, and she accepts his kindness, which leads him to both inquire about Gale and to suggest that his father knew her mother once upon a time.

When Katniss arrives in her room, she finds the red-headed girl tidying up. Her guilt returns but she knows it would be dangerous to apologize out loud to the girl, who she realizes probably despises her for having not intervened on that day long ago.

ANALYSIS

The meticulousness with which the spectacle of the Games is built becomes apparent in these chapters. The idea of characterizing tributes through design speaks to the vacuousness of the spectacle – it is, in effect, a "reality show" where reality is a deliberately designed illusion. This is not at all dissimilar to our own reality shows, so it serves as a social critique. The fanfare that greets them provides a great irony for Katniss, since she finds herself excited by the very elements she ought to disdain. She is excited to be in a position she detests.

In terms of class, Katniss is aware that the design process usually continues to penalize those of lower social station, since District 12 tributes tend to be decorated in an unflattering coal motif. Cinna's masterstroke is to emphasize the individual in his tributes, rather than generalize them into their class. While it should be noted that his fire strategy is very much a play to the spectacle of the Games, it also allows them to have an identity that is about *them*, rather than about where they are from and what industry their parents are engaged in. The theme of class is also seen in these chapters as the luxury continues to increase and overwhelm Katniss.

The design specifically gives Katniss an identity that holds metaphoric significance – "the girl who was on fire." Fire, traditionally a metaphor for consuming passion, is something that does not define Katniss, a stoic hero, at this point, but does set her up for her growth into a fuller person who can accept emotion.

But her stoic front is very much on display in these chapters, even as it comes in conflict with Haymitch's strategy of selling her and Peeta as a unified front. Peeta gives her plenty of reason to trust him – both in the past through the bread incident, and in these chapters through lying for her when she recognizes the Avox - but she cannot see him as an ally unless she is able to understand it as a functional advantage. The idea of selflessly trusting someone is too foreign to her, as she is so accustomed to working alone.

This all plays into the theme of community and revolution, which manifests in these chapters in two ways. First, the aforementioned strategy of presenting a unified front. Katniss's confusion about this, whereas Peeta easily accepts it, indicates her inability to yet understand the comfort of trust. But the more intense manifestation involves the red-headed Avox. Katniss has a deep ambivalence about the incident she relates, where she and Gale refused to sacrifice themselves for the girl in the woods. While it made functional sense to stay hidden, Katniss battles a feeling that she showed weakness by not sacrificing herself for the girls' safety, an indication of the mindset she will continue to develop through the novel. Also note that Avox is built from the Latin [I]a (a negation prefix) and [I]vox (voice).

Lastly, the introduction of President Snow suggests that Panem operates under the guise of a democracy – he is President, after all. It's one of the traditional dystopic ironies, a government of the people that is hardly operating in those people's best interests.

Summary and Analysis of Chapter 7-9

CHAPTER SEVEN

Katniss awakes from nightmares to find she has bitten the side of her mouth and tastes a bit of her blood. After a breakfast in her room, she dons her appointed outfit and then discovers Peeta has been dressed similarly again. They are led together to their first training session with Haymitch, where they decide they will train together for their first stage. Tributes are trained by their mentors for three days before training with all the tributes at once, culminating in a private session with the Gamemakers, who design and execute each year's contest.

Haymitch inquires further into their abilities, and each child accuses the other of downplaying his or her abilities – Peeta is convinced Katniss's hunting skills are formidable, and she praises his strength. Haymitch warns them to keep their skills a secret from other tributes, and also stresses that they should continue to stay by each other's sides. Katniss isn't certain whether Peeta meant his protestations about her abilities as evidence of his affection or contempt, and she lashes out at him.

The next day, they are both led to the basement training gymnasium, which is organized into several training stations. Each tribute is given a cloth square with his or her district number on it, though only Katniss and Peeta are dressed in tandem. The representative, Atala, explains that children can move from station to station at will, but cannot fight one another. This occasion provides Katniss's first glimpse at the other tributes, and she sees that though she is smaller, she is healthier than most – with the exception of the group she calls "the Careers." They are tributes from richer districts who are trained from birth with the expectation they will compete in the Games. This group in particular seems to regard her with contempt.

Following Haymitch's instructions, Peeta and Katniss avoid the heavy-duty skill tables, and instead focus on knot-tying and camouflage, the latter of which proves to come naturally to Peeta. Over the next three days, they continue to train while avoiding archery and weightlifting. All the while, Katniss feels annoyed with Peeta but they maintain the image of a unified front even as no one else talks to them. During their time, she learns that the little girl from District 12 is named Rue and notices Rue seems interested in them. Also, she continues to keep Peeta at an emotional distance, even if they pretend otherwise by staying together.

On the third day, they are called individually from a group lunch to audition before the Gamemakers, where they will be judged via a number score that will communicate their talents to sponsors. As the female tribute from the last District, Katniss is called last and immediately notices that the Gamemakers, who have been there all day and endured 23 previous displays, are drunk and distracted. She has some trouble with the more professional bows available, but eventually begins to display her aptitude at archery. Their indifference to her work, manifested in their attention to a newly-arrived roasted pig, angers her and she fires an arrow directly to their balcony, skewering the apple in the pig's mouth with her arrow. She knows it was a mistake and leaves immediately.

CHAPTER EIGHT

Distraught, Katniss takes to her room, ignoring Haymitch and Effie's requests to talk to her, since she is convinced that her assuredly low score will engender her death through a lack of sponsorship. Finally, she acquiesces and joins her team at dinner. When she confesses the truth, Haymitch admits it will cost her but does assuage her worries that her impetuousness will affect her family back home.

They watch the scores reported on the television. Again, scores are awarded at 1-12. The Careers got their expected 8-10, the little Rue gets a surprising 7, Peeta gets a respectable 8, but the great news is that Katniss gets an 11.

The next morning, Katniss remembers meeting Gale. They met while hunting separately in the woods, and she knew him only as another boy whose father had died in the explosion that took her own. They built a trust and friendship over time to become, finally, a team. In thinking of the importance of having a partner, she for the first time compares gentle, middle-class Peeta to handy, lower-class Gale. The next morning, she is reminded by Effie that they must prepare for her televised interview that will take place the next night. But the big news is that Peeta has informed Haymitch that he would like to be coached separately from that point onwards.

CHAPTER NINE

Katniss is torn over Peeta's decision, uncertain why she feels personally betrayed by his decision, but relieved that she can no longer feel compelled to pretend a friendship. Her first four hours of interview prep involve a type of finishing school with Effie – how to walk in high heels, to sit lady-like, to smile, etc.

She and Peeta then change mentors, and she and Haymitch begin strategizing what she should talk about in the interview. He is worried her natural hostility will hurt her in the interview, but they cannot find an attitude that she can pull off effectively, so intense is her contempt for both her mentor and the situation itself.

Full of anger, she smashes plates in her room until the red-headed Avox arrives and surprisingly treats her gently. Katniss whispers an apology but the Avox suggests she did not act inappropriately. They clean the room together and then the Avox tucks her in.

The next day, Cinna and the prep team work hard preparing her for the interview, continuing their fire motif both through costume, stencils, a shimmering skin powder, and most impressively, a dress made of reflective fiery gems. She is enamored of her appearance, and confesses her attitude problem to Cinna, who then suggests she bypass her contempt for the crowd by pretending she is answering all the questions to him personally.

She and Peeta, also dressed in the fire motif, are led out to a stage with the other tributes. Haymitch reminds them to keep up the appearance of a happy pair. She realizes how many people are watching, both live and on TV, when she recognizes the familiar face of Caesar Flickerman, the interview host of over 40 years who has maintained a youthful façade through surgery. Renowned for his affability, he is able through his manner to assuage her stage fright before she goes up, second-to-last. Through the use of Cinna's strategy, she presents herself with charm and honesty, earning in the process both laughs and admiration from the audience. Her crowning moment is when she twirls in her dress and giggles endearingly.

Though a mention of Prim drives her back to her tense hatred, she makes it through the interview well and sits to watch Peeta. His natural charm with a crowd impresses her, but the biggest shock is when he confesses to Caesar that he has always had a crush on Katniss.

ANALYSIS

Katniss finds herself in these chapters torn over how to interpret Peeta's friendliness. She grows increasingly hostile to him, because his seeming genuine kindness is irreconcilable with her determination to not let emotions interfere with her will to survive (which of course will ultimately mean killing him). She pushes him away, but nevertheless is torn by her emotional sense of betrayal when he asks to train separately. And already, it is becoming clear to the reader that Peeta seems to really like her – something she can't let herself recognize in the midst of her inner turmoil. The spectacle proves useful to her in terms of this, since the unified front strategy gives her a way to explain to herself why she stays close to him.

But her emotions, as well as her revolutionary zeal, are starting to surface in force. This is most apparent with the Gamemakers, when she grows indignant at their disinterest in her. Her anger has been turned towards a higher authority and not just against her fellow tributes – a sign of individual defiance and one hardly lacking in emotional weight. It makes sense that she cries for the first time after this. Instead of being punished for her emotional transgression, though, she finds it brings reward in the shape of her 11 score. Throughout her time in the arena, she will find that displays of emotion, rather than stoic commitment, bring rewards.

It is worth considering how her feelings for Peeta are complicated by class resentments. It's an indirect theme in these chapters – Katniss rarely frames it in this way – but it is implicit in her comparisons of Peeta and Gale. Peeta certainly has a spark and is not utterly compliant – he stands up to her and their mentors, albeit with less force than she does. And yet she thinks of him as being "softer" than Gale – his middle class life as a baker's son has not given him a certain strength she expects, a strength that she finds in Gale, who knows a life of scrounging.

There is one nice passage in these chapters that indicates how Katniss reflects on how their poverty significantly shapes their values in contrast to the vacuousness of the Capitol cronies. On pages 124-125, she considers how Caesar Flickerman's perpetually youthful appearance, due to plastic surgery, is in stark contrast to the Seam value of honoring signs of age, since they indicate one who has managed to survive against the odds.

Summary and Analysis of Chapters 10-11

CHAPTER TEN (START OF PART TWO)

Katniss immediately endeavors to hide her emotions, even though the crowd shows great support for this new development. She avoids Peeta until they are back on their floor, at which point she shoves him into some plants that shatter and hurt his hands. Haymitch arrives and diffuses the situation, arguing that Peeta's declaration only helps her case by making her look desirable and attractive to sponsors.

Once they are reunited at dinner, Peeta's hands are bandaged and Katniss curses that she owes him yet again. After watching their replay on TV, which Katniss acknowledges to herself was effective, they must say their good-byes until the games begin the next day. Effie thanks them, and then Haymitch gives them his final advice: when the gong sounds, run away from the group and make water first priority.

That night, Katniss decides to keep her fingernails flame-painted and then, for the first time, wears the Capitol-given nightgown to sleep. But despite needing to rest for the sake of her strength, she can't sleep. She goes out to the roof, where she finds Peeta lost in thought. When he confesses to her that he knows he can't win but wants to die "as himself" – that is, without having had his morality compromised by the Game – Katniss is shamed by his purity and transfers it to contempt. There are no rules in the arena, she convinces herself, and he will certainly compromise himself eventually, as she plans to do in order to survive.

The next morning, she is brought up to a hovercraft on the roof, where she is implanted via syringe with a tracking device so the Gamekeepers can keep her story televised. After a half hour ride and a final nice breakfast, Katniss is lowered into underground quarters for final preparation in what is called the "Launch Room." After a shower, she is dressed in the tribute outfit, a simple get-up that all tributes will wear. Cinna surprises her by giving her the mockingjay pin she had forgotten. Cinna tenderly comforts her until she is lifted by glass cylinder up to the surface, where she is blinded by the light and surprised by the voice of the famous announcer, Claudius Templesmith, as he welcomes everyone to the 74th Hunger Games.

CHAPTER 11

Each tribute stands on his or her own metal circle, all equidistant from the "Cornucopia," an oversized golden horn in the middle of the field, overflowing with supplies including food and weapons. Other tools are spread throughout the field. The rule (pretty much the only one) states that tributes must wait 60 seconds before a gong allows them to step off, or they will be blown up by land mines. After that begins the "bloodbath," wherein tributes rush for supplies and enter their first skirmishes.

Katniss uses her minute to take in her surroundings. On one end of their plain, the ground seems to drop off. On one side is a lake, and on another the border of sparse woodland. Haymitch's advice suggests she should eschew any supplies and rush into the woods in search for water. But she is likewise tempted to compete for the boons, which include a bow and arrow she believes must have been left for her. She is undecided and looks over to Peeta, several metal circles over, but her inability to read what he is trying to tell her proves distracting, and she is not ready to make a sprint when the gong is struck.

Therefore, she gives up on the plan to rush for the Cornucopia and instead grabs an orange backpack near her. Another boy arrives at the same time but before they can fight, he spits blood in her face and she sees he has been killed via a knife in his back. A girl from District 2 (later identified as Clove), is revealed as the killer proficient with throwing knives. Katniss rushes immediately towards the woods, and her instincts lead her to lift her bag to protect her head, which gains her a knife that otherwise would have killed her. Before she rushes into the woods, she turns to see several tributes fighting at the Cornucopia and several others reduced to corpses in the field.

For several hours, she continues to move through the woods. She is happy to see rabbits, since they promise not only game to be hunted later, but also the existence of a water source other than the lake near the starting field. All the while, she's aware that she could well be on TV. Hours later, she hears the first shots of the cannon, each shot of which signifies the death of a tribute.

Once she's far enough removed to justify rest, she examines the contents of her backpack to find: some small non-perishable foods; a sleeping bag designed for the cold; some iodine for treating water; a pair of sunglasses; and other survival supplies. Meanwhile, she is beginning to register the symptoms of her thirst, and fears dehydration.

Nighttime comes, and after setting some snares, she protects herself by climbing up into a tree that her bigger opponents could never scale even if they did see her. She rigs herself safely so she can sleep, and from that vantage watches the nightly recap. Each night, the Panem anthem plays and then images of that day's dead tributes are broadcast into the sky. She is relieved that Peeta's face is not among them. Of those still alive are also the five "Career" kids, a girl she has dubbed "Foxface," an extremely large boy named Thresh, and the little girl, Rue.

It is cold at night, and her sleeping bag is crucial to keeping her comfortable. She is able to sleep but is woken by the sound of snapping branches nearby. She realizes that someone is building a fire, an extremely stupid mistake that soon attracts the Career tributes, who she sees have formed an alliance, not uncommon for the early stages of the games. After hearing the fire-maker's screams, the Careers gather nearby and are surprised not to hear a cannon. They wonder if they'd effectively killed the girl, and argue until one of them volunteers to go back and finish her off.

Katniss's biggest shock, however, is to realize that it's Peeta who made that offer.

ANALYSIS

These are some of the most exciting chapters from an adventure standpoint, since they reveal for the first time Katniss's honed survival instincts in their full glory.

All the while, Katniss's conflict between stoic detachment and her emotions continues to escalate. Obviously, her confusion about Peeta's motives has never been greater than after his confession to Caeser Flickerman. And after his roof-top confession, she doesn't know how to understand his sensitivity as divorced from a possible tactical value. What's happening is she dislikes herself for her survival stoicism but is unable to manage that insight and so lashes out at him instead. She feels almost vindicated when she believes he has allied himself with the Careers, but still harbors the lingering sadness of perceived betrayal. In other words, her emotions are getting harder to control – symbolized by her desire to keep her fingernails painted with the flame design.

The flame design also speaks to the ever-increasing revolutionary zeal. Peeta's confessed desire to die "as himself" really cuts Katniss to the quick, since she had settled on a stoic detachment from her fellow tributes. Though it doesn't register for a while, Peeta's idealism speaks to her nascent revolutionary zeal, an indignation that makes the Capitol her antagonist, and her community her allies.

She will even play to the spectacle. Her awareness of the potential audience that could be watching her grows evermore important to her. The brutality of the games is becoming more apparent to the reader with glimpses of how manipulated the Game is for entertainment value.

Significant naming continues in this section. Important people associated with the running of the Games have explicitly Roman names - Caesar Flickerman, Claudius Templesmith, Seneca Crane, and, in later books, Plutarch Heavensbee. In the case of Caesar and Claudius, their surnames also describe their work. It is a graceful naming convention, thematically tying the Capitol's gamemakers to the Romans, while contrasting with the District 12 names that tend to sound like plants and flowers.

Summary and Analysis of Chapters 12-14

CHAPTER TWELVE

Katniss is both shocked and disgusted to see her fellow tribute ally himself with the "Capitol's lapdogs." When Peeta goes back to finish the girl, she overhears that the other Careers are not overly impressed with him but rather are using him in hopes that he can help them find her. Their contempt is specifically directed towards her.

Soon after, she hears the cannon and a hovercraft arrives to take the body of the dead tribute. The next morning, she hunts and catches a rabbit, using the dead girl's dying fire to cook it. She's well aware that audiences are watching, and makes sure she is presenting herself and her abilities well so as to attract sponsors.

She continues to move downhill, but is beginning to suffer from her lack of water. She finds berries, but cannot remember from her training whether they might be toxic. Though she has food, her strength is wavering. She prays Haymitch will send her water via sponsors, even speaking the word aloud so as to capture it on camera. No luck. Consumed with anger and dehydration, she is unsure whether she can go on until she realizes perhaps Haymitch has refused her water because he knows she's already near it.

When she finds mud, she knows she's close, and follows it to a pond. She collects water in her flask and treats it so she can have her first hydration in days. All is well as she hooks herself into a tree that night. All is not well when she awakes suddenly in the night to find a "wall of fire descending" on her.

CHAPTER THIRTEEN

There is fire everywhere, and Katniss acts quickly by leaping to the ground. She knows immediately what has happened – occasionally, when the Games are not entertaining enough, the Gamemakers will engineer occasions to spice things up. This includes climate modification within the arena.

The fire is bad enough, but worse is the smoke, which is ravaging her lungs and forcing her to vomit. She is about to change her plan, to move parallel to the flame and avoid it, when fireballs are launched directly at her. She keeps her head and is able to avoid most of the fireballs, but one finally makes contact with her calf, burning it badly.

As the sun begins to rise, she escapes the flame area and treats herself in a nearby pool of water. Her hands have been burnt but the real damage is to her calf, now covered with blisters. The water helps alleviate the pain somewhat, but she knows she will need more sophisticated healing than is at her command. The intensity of pain and her drowsiness from dealing with the smoke paralyzes her, on top of which she is scared to leave the water that provides temporary relief.

That is, paralyzes her until she hears the Careers approaching. She rushes up into the highest tree she can find, managing the pain on her palms as she climbs. When she looks down, she sees the five careers and Peeta staring up her way. Where Peeta avoids her gaze, Glimmer hands the bow and arrow – which she has claimed from the Cornucopia – to Cato, one of the Careers. He turns it down and unsheathes his sword before attempting to climb after her. It's not long before he falls back down, after which Glimmer attempts to climb and shoot her. No luck. Finally, Peeta tells them they should just wait her out, since there's nowhere she can go.

She belts herself in, scared and weak from hunger. Across the way, up in another tree, she recognizes two eyes watching her through the dark. It's Rue, who points to something over Katniss's head.

CHAPTER FOURTEEN

Katniss looks up at Rue's gesture to see a wasp nest above her. She worries that these aren't normal wasps but one of the Capitol's muttations, "tracker jackers." These muttations were designed as weapons during the war. When they sting someone, he suffers severe hallucinations and sometimes death.

Though frightened by the possibility, she realizes that any wasp nest could prove a boon if she can saw its branch off and send the nest down to the Careers who are waiting for her below. In order not to alert them with the sound of sawing, she decides to wait for the nightly anthem to use the music as disguise. She climbs up as far away as she can, and realizes the smoke of the recent firestorm has subdued the usually frenetic wasps. As the anthem blares, she does her best but the pain in her hands limits her effectiveness and she doesn't finish. She decides to return to her sleeping spot and wait until dawn to finish the sawing.

Back at her bedspot, she finds her first gift from a sponsor, which has been dropped from the sky with a silver parachute attached. It is ointment she uses to alleviate the pain of her burns. She settles to sleep but awakes in the early dawn, and sees the Careers (with Peeta) asleep below. Before resuming her sawing, she looks over to Rue, who is still in the tree next door, and silently warns her. As Rue escapes through the trees, she realizes that the little girl is surviving by leaping from tree to tree. Up close to the nest, Katniss sees the wasps are less subdued than before. She moves quickly and is able to saw through the branch, but not before being stung three times, on her knee, cheek, and neck.

But her pains are little compared to what happens below, where the nest explodes and the wasps attack the Careers. They flee quickly to the Lake, but Glimmer's flight is ceded by stings and she falls to the ground. Katniss drops from the tree and returns to her pool, where she pulls the stingers from her skin. Nevertheless, her injuries have swollen and are emitting pus. But Katniss has no time to relax, since she realizes that Glimmer's fall means the bow is now available. She rushes over to find that her severe stings have paralyzed her body so that Katniss must break her fingers in order to free the bow. What's more, as she tries to pull it free, Glimmer's flesh begins to disintegrate in her hands.

That's when she realizes that the hallucinations engendered by the tracker jackers have begun. She frees the bow just about the time that some of the Careers return. She readies herself to fire but lacks lucidity from the hallucinations, and is unprepared when Peeta comes upon her. Yet not only does he make no effort to kill her, but he in fact insists she run away. As she stands to do so, Cato enters the clearing, and she sees he has been stung under the eye.

She rushes away, running as best she can through hallucinations and trying not to lose herself. But one thing is crystal clear – that Peeta has saved her life.

ANALYSIS

Peeta's seeming betrayal helps Katniss to direct her fury back at her antagonists in the arena. Again, there are undertones of class resentment in her hatred of the Career Tributes, by the disgust she feels for children privileged enough to devote their lives to training for this event. Her aptitude for the Games has been shaped by necessity and never directed. One can also ask the question why, faced with her high score, they wouldn't have proposed she ally with them? Could their particular hatred of her be motivated by her low social standing?

Regardless, Katniss is able to redouble her dedication to stoically surviving now that she can disregard Peeta's confession about wanting to survive "as himself." For these chapters, at least, she is convinced she will persist without trusting anyone.

The spectacle continues to play itself out, as the wall of fire is another step of complete manipulation meant to keep audiences entertained. In the sense that our reality TV shows are actually scripted, so is the "reality" of this game not really relevant.

Finally, these chapters provide something the novel has lacked thus far: a clear, identifiable antagonist for Katniss. Once she identifies Cato in these scenes, he continues to personify the forces of the cruel Careers for the reader, even as Katniss's sense of antagonism continues to be progressively more directed towards the people up top.

Summary and Analysis of Chapters 15-18

CHAPTER FIFTEEN

The tracker jacker stings lead her into intense nightmares in which she confronts all of her worst fears – namely, that those she means to protect are punished. Finally, she awakes to find herself in a shallow hole, having slept for what she believes was at least a full day or two. As she tries to assuage her parched tongue, she thinks of Gale and wonders why Peeta would have saved her. For the first time, she realizes how different the two boys truly are. Her one pleasure at this point is that she's now found herself with a bow.

She's in bad shape, what with her weight loss, her burns, and her wounds, but the most important goal is to hydrate herself. She moves slowly through the woods, killing a rabbit and finally finding a stream. She eats a bit of the food from her pack and then continues to move, for the first time uphill. In the afternoon, she risks a fire to cook a bird she's shot, but as she prepares it, she hears a twig snap and recognizes Rue hiding nearby.

She calls out offering to form an alliance, an offer Rue accepts quickly. Rue, a tribute from the agricultural District 11, knows how to cure Katniss's stings. She finds some particular leaves and chews them up, after which they provide great relief when placed over the wounds. In return, Katniss uses her lotion on Rue's burn. They pool their food for a dinner, and while Katniss realizes the foolishness of forming an alliance with someone she will ultimately have to kill, she is pleased to have a friend. As they talk, Rue explains to Katniss how in District 11, they grow crops for all of Panem but are not allowed to eat them themselves. Katniss wonders if the television broadcast is blocking out their conversation so as not to reveal to any district how other districts work.

They spend some time comparing their respective supplies, and Rue explains that the sunglasses from Katniss's pack, which she found weird to wear in sunlight, are actually night-vision glasses. As Katniss had slept through the previous night's casualty announcement, Rue tells her there are 10 tributes left. What's more, she has been spying on the Career camp and has some information. They have camped out alongside the lake and Cornucopia, living off its supplies. What's more, Peeta is no longer with them.

When the night comes, Katniss offers to share her sleeping bag with Rue, an offer Rue gladly accepts. But before they go to sleep, Katniss pieces together that maybe the Careers won't be so well off without their supplies and proposes for the first time that maybe her best defense would be a strong offense.

CHAPTER SIXTEEN

Katniss reasons that her poverty might work to her advantage, since it has taught her to survive without resources, where the Careers lack hunting skills and are thus dependent on the Cornucopia. She begins to think how she'll destroy their food, when she falls asleep. The next morning, the cannon fires, signifying another death and waking Katniss.

After a breakfast of eggs that Rue gathered alongside some rabbit and berries, Katniss grills Rue for more details about the Career camp. Rue tells her that they have been hunting during the day, leaving a boy from District 3 to guard the supplies. This confuses Katniss, since the boy in question is not very big. Katniss intuits that there is an uncertain element about the situation, which leaves her unclear on how she might destroy the supplies.

Katniss and Rue gather berries and greens together, and Katniss learns about her new ally. In District 11, foraging is much more difficult than in District 12, mainly because the 11 Peacekeepers are more aggressive. Rue's great pleasure is music, and she tells how during the harvest, she stays up in the trees so as to see the flag signifying quitting time. When she sees it, she hums a tune that mockingjays (District 11 has its fair share) then repeat through the fields so that all of the harvesters know they can quit for the day. Realizing how much Rue values mockingjays, Katniss offers her the gold pin, but Rue insists Katniss keep it.

After lunch, the girls devise a plan. They will set up three campfires, which Rue will then light at intervals to distract the Careers so Katniss can destroy the Cornucopia. As a means of communication, Rue teaches Katniss her harvest whistle and they agree to send the message via mockingjays in case either is delayed on her way to the rendezvous point. Before they part, Rue hugs Katniss, an emotional move that calls Prim to her mind.

As Katniss heads towards the Careers camp, she wonders whether Peeta was attacked for helping her, or whether the whole thing was just a hallucination. She makes it to a spot Rue indicated that allows her to survey them. Along with Cato and two others is the small boy. They are camped around the Cornucopia, which has been drained of supplies. The supplies now sit covered by a net, a good distance away from the Cornucopia. Katniss is confused and wondering what she's missing when she sees Cato point out to the woods. Rue has lit the first fire.

They begin to argue loudly, and Katniss hears one ask about "Lover Boy." Cato indicates he's no concern – "I know where I cut him" – and says his main goal is to find and kill a girl who Katniss assumes means her. They all leave, including the guard.

Katniss waits a while, still wondering how to pull this off. She considers launching flaming arrows, but it would likely fail and give away both her position and a precious arrow. Suddenly, someone rushes out from the woods – it's the girl tribute who Katniss nicknamed "Foxface." She shows her wily nature as she arrives near the supplies and strangely begins to hop closer and closer to them. She arrives at them, fills her pack, and then escapes the same way. Katniss then pieces it together – the boy from District 3, the factory district, must have knowledge of electronics and used it to reactivate the mines that initially kept tributes on their metal circles at Game's beginning. This explains why the Careers would value such a small boy, and why they would be willing to leave the supplies out in the open.

As she sees the smoke from Rue's second fire, she still lacks a plan. Then she notices a burlap sack of apples up top, and devises one. It takes her three arrows, but she is able to rip the bag open, causing the apples to slip down the pile and all over the ground, which then causes an explosion that blows her backwards into the air.

CHAPTER SEVENTEEN

Katniss is slammed hard against the ground, and has to manage both shrapnel and smoke. She knows escape is crucial but lacks the composure to do so immediately. In addition to her shortness of breath, her left ear is bleeding and she can hear from neither ear. And lastly, she wants to avoid looking weak for the audiences.

Her only option is to crawl, which she does. Two belated explosions slow her down, but she makes it back to the bushes right as Cato and his crew return. Cato exhibits a petulant anger while the others try to find any supplies to salvage from the ruined pile. There is nothing, which prompts Cato to break the District 3 boy's neck.

Katniss has to pass the day in the bushes, and at night everyone sees the post-anthem images, which show the Careers that whoever blew up their pile did not die in the explosion. They light some torches, put on their own night-vision sunglasses, and take off after whoever it was, not knowing she's watching them. A while later, Katniss risks heading to the lake to drink and to clean herself. Though her sunglasses give her night vision, she still cannot hear. When she stops to sleep, she remembers she left her sleeping bag with Rue and thus must brave the cold night.

She is woken the next morning by Foxface's laugh as Foxface surveys the wreckage. She realizes that destroyed supplies mean advantage for the non-Careers. Katniss considers offering her alliance, but refrains. She realizes she can hear out of her right ear, though her left is still non-functional.

A while later, Katniss decides to head back along the stream. She kills some fish and groosling, and takes off her boots to keep from leaving a trail. Rue is not at their rendezvous spot, but there is no mockingjay sign and so Katniss does not worry yet. What concerns her more is a growing hunger, which her meager food does not sate.

Once it becomes late afternoon and Rue has still not returned, Katniss heads out to the spot where the third fire, which Rue never set off to her knowledge, was supposed to be. She decides to search for Rue, who she assumes is up in a tree hiding from a threat, and appreciates the compulsion to be active. Finally, she hears Rue's melody repeated through the mockingjays. She follows the sound until it is eclipsed by Rue's scream through the trees, which leads Katniss to rush out to a clearing where Rue is entangled in a net. She calls Katniss's name right before a spear is thrust into her body.

CHAPTER EIGHTEEN

Rue's killer is the boy from District 1, who Katniss kills via arrow right away. She rushes to Rue and realizes the girl's wound is too severe to be healed. As she dies, she asks Katniss to sing to her, something Katniss has not done since her father died. But the connection she's made between Rue and Prim is affecting, and she emotionally sings a song that the mockingjays then repeat throughout the woods.

Katniss is full of rage against the Capitol for facilitating such cruelty, and she thinks of what Peeta told her on the roof, that he hoped to die in such a way that the Capitol knew they do not own him. As a small rebellion, Katniss decorates Rue's body with flowers, a type of funeral that is antithetical to the murderous raison d'etre of the Games, even though she knows they'll never allow that detail to be aired on TV. She touches three fingers to her lips and raises her arm to Rue's body as it is removed, using a traditional District 12 salute.

After an emotional goodbye to Rue, she leaves the clearing feeling full of hatred. As she is about to make camp in a tree, another sponsor gift comes down. In it, she finds a loaf of bread, the type of bread specifically grown in District 11. She realizes it is a gesture of appreciation from Rue's district, particularly poignant since gifts are extremely expensive and the district is poor.

Committed to a new aggressive hunting strategy, Katniss first gets herself food. She risks making a fire, partially hoping it will draw Cato out but not surprised it does not. She wonders if maybe they think Thresh, who was also from District 11, was the one who avenged Rue's death and not her. For the first time, Katniss begins to believe she has a chance to win the Games, not only because the playing field has been leveled but because she is enlivened by the desire for revenge. It is only at this point that Katniss realizes that she has committed her first kill.

That evening, instead of the anthem, a series of trumpets are played. These traditionally indicate a message for the tributes, usually an invitation to a "feast," meant to draw hungry tributes together and encourage bloodbath to entertain the folks at home. But the announcement, spoken by Claudius Templesmith, is not a feast invitation but a change in the rules: for the first time in Games history, the two tributes from any particular district can win together. Katniss doesn't have to kill Peeta.

Instinctively, she screams out his name.

ANALYSIS

Peeta's kindness yet again challenges Katniss's stoicism. She insists to herself that she is committed to the murderous reality of the Games, but she is becoming less able to hide it from her reader. She continues to remind herself that she will have to kill Rue at some point, but it's clear enough that she would not, since her connection to Rue is as much emotional as tactical.

In fact, her stoic dedication is put to the test soon after when she allies with Rue. She considers to herself the tactical advantage of the alliance even as it is abundantly clear that she is desperate for friendship, and the girl she associates with Prim is a perfect companion. As Prim was seen to be a personification of Katniss's childish innocence in the early chapters, her immediate embrace of Rue as ally illustrates the journey towards shaping her identity as a girl defined by individual moral choices and not just survival. Also note that Collins' clever naming continues with Rue. The plant rue is associated in poetry with sadness, regret, and grace. In mythology, the basilisk has no effect on rue (and indeed the arena has little effect on the girl Rue). Finally, the plant rue is an insect repellant.

However, she doesn't fully realize her emotional connection to Rue until the young girl dies. Her song is genuine, not forced by awareness of the audience, and her flower decorations exhibit both her realizations about her identity and her burgeoning rebellion. In terms of the revolutionary theme, Katniss considers the flowers to be an act of individual rebellion against the Capitol. It can only hurt her chances in the arena, but she is asserting herself to be not controlled by them – in effect, understanding the meaning of Peeta's roof confession. Additionally, this episode illustrates Katniss's acceptance of her identity – she is a girl who values other people's dignity, and not just a competitor willing to accept their rules to survive. As happened before, she is rewarded for this selflessness with a gift, this time from District 11. One other episode illustrating her growing sense of values is when she sees Cato snap the engineer boy's neck – by confronting the brutality honestly, she is learning what she will not let herself become.

The image of the mockingjay is fleshed out in these chapters – it's a bird that reproduces music (a symbol of emotion for Katniss, who relates it to her father), producing beauty by working in tandem with its brethren. The way in which it represents Katniss's acceptance of community will continue to resonate.

After Rue's death, her hatred increases for the Capitol and it becomes a more distinct antagonist. Nevertheless, she does continue to play the spectacle through these chapters, worrying about showing the true extent of her physical pain after the mine-field explosion because of audiences. For all of her growth, she still has a survival instinct that keeps her hardened to the suffering in the arena. This stoic determination flounders when she learns she can ally with Peeta, and then loses herself into a cry for him.

Summary and Analysis of Chapters 19-22

CHAPTER NINETEEN (START OF PART THREE)

This new rule is obviously meant specially for Katniss. She wonders whether Peeta's love angle has been designed to get audiences to demand an arrangement of this sort. She decides to further pursue that angle, and smiles for the cameras.

The next morning, she sets out carefully, knowing the Careers will be on the look-out. Her only lead is knowing Peeta, who Cato believes is cut badly, must have established himself somewhere near a water source. Katniss sets a fire to distract the Careers and sets off to some of the distant water. At some point, she finds a bloody trail that she follows along a stream. But it's another dead end, or at least she thinks so before Peeta's voice comes from nowhere.

She looks down into the stream and his eyes open from the mud. He has used his camouflage talent to hide himself. She gives him some water and he tells her he has indeed been cut, high up his left thigh. His wound and weakness prove problematic when Katniss is unable to easily pull him out from his hiding spot. She yanks at him, but his cries deter her. Little by little, she rolls him out and then she sets to cleaning him.

His wounds are bad. He's badly burnt, has four tracker jacker stings, and a bad fever which Katniss addresses with some pills from her pack. But most grievous of all is his leg cut, which is deep, inflamed, and obviously infected. The intensity reminds Katniss of how, when her mother has been brought seriously injured patients, Katniss rushed away, unable to handle the gruesomeness.

She tries to hide her fear over his wound, but doesn't know what she can do about it with her limited supplies. She uses the leaves remedy Rue taught her, to minimal effect. Meanwhile, Peeta is jokingly begging her to give him a kiss, since they are expected to be in love. Peeta seems a bit upset when he learns that Katniss has been given gifts whereas he hasn't, but claims not to be surprised since he believes she is Haymitch's favorite.

They head down the stream together, moving extremely slowly because of Peeta's wounds. Finally, she sees some rocks forming a cave and carries him to it. In the cave, she makes a bed for Peeta and does the best she can to disguise the opening. Peeta tries to talk to her about arrangements in case he dies, but in order to shut him up, she kisses him. It works. It's also her first kiss.

When she steps outside for air, a silver parachute drops. She hopes it's infection medicine, but it's only a pot of broth. She believes she understands Haymitch's point: "one kiss equals one pot of broth," since it pleases the audience. If she wants more, she'll have to give them more.

CHAPTER TWENTY

Through the use of argument and kisses, she slowly gets Peeta to eat the broth. Realizing she can't leave to hunt since they're so close to the stream where she found him (and they left signs), she sits on watch. When it gets too cold, she crawls into the sleeping bag with him. She isn't certain allying with Peeta was the right move, since she's now more vulnerable than before, but she trusts her instincts.

The next morning, his fever has broken. He is extremely sweet to her, which she admires since it plays to the audience. He demands she sleep and let him take watch and, exhausted, she agrees. When she wakes later that afternoon, she tends his wounds and discovers his leg has significantly worsened, suggesting blood poisoning.

Katniss heads out to gather some greens, noticing how hot it's gotten. She believes the Gamemakers must be increasing the temperature. With everything she gathers, she prepares a pot of stew and leaves it to cook in the intense heat. She also sets snares in hopes of catching game, since she is too worried about leaving Peeta alone for the length of a hunt.

She finds Peeta resting and sickly, and he asks for a story. Unable to think of anything that doesn't involve Gale (the idea of bringing Gale up to Peeta makes her nervous), she decides to tell him about how she found Prim's goat Lady.

The story she tells him leaves out details that could potentially incriminate her or Gale for poaching outside the District borders, but she reveals to her reader the full story. On Prim's tenth birthday, she was hoping for an extra-lucrative hunt so as to trade for a present. Luckily, she and Gale saw a nice-sized deer, which she killed, making her feel guilty. But the meat sold well, and with the money, Katniss made an offer to the "goat man" to buy one of his wounded goats, which he planned otherwise to sell for meat. The goat's wound seemed terminal, but when Katniss brought it to her healer mother and Prim, they were overjoyed to get right to work patching it up, and Prim loved it.

Peeta praises Katniss's kindness even as Katniss tries to downplay it. He promises to show the same gratitude for saving his life that Lady the goat did. As she tries to lower his fever, the trumpets blare again. This time, Claudius Templesmith is indeed inviting the tributes to come together, not for an ordinary feast, but for a gathering where each of them can get what he or she "desperately" needs. Assuming that she will find anti-infection medicine there, Katniss plans to go, but Peeta demands she promise not to risk her life for him again.

They eat the soup as Katniss plots how she can get him asleep long enough to escape, knowing he is serious enough to potentially try and follow her. She comes on no solution until, while gathering water at the stream, a silver parachute comes down. It's not infection medicine, but sleep syrup, which she takes as a rather cruel choice on Haymitch's part. But the message is clear enough, and so she mixes the syrup with some berries and uses the concoction to knock Peeta out.

CHAPTER TWENTY-ONE

After significantly camouflaging the cave opening and gathering a supply of food and water to leave Peeta, Katniss curls next to him to sleep, very frightened since feasts always end up with corpses. She thinks of how school is probably cancelled back home at this late point of the Games, and wonders whether there is a simmering romance between her and Gale.

The night is extremely cold when she decides to take off, using Peeta's jacket and Rue's socks to further warm herself. Before she leaves, she gives Peeta a long kiss, to please the audiences. She heads out, worried her bum ear will betray her. Once she arrives near the clearing, she sees neither anybody waiting nor any gifts. She waits till the morning comes, at which point a round table with several bags lifts from the ground. Each bag has a number pinned on it, indicating for which district the particular gift is intended. The District 12 gift is a small bag, which she acknowledges she could fit around her wrist.

Before anyone can make a move, Foxface darts from the Cornucopia itself, where she was obviously hiding, and sprints out into the woods, grabbing her gift on the way. Admiring the ingenuity but aware that the next step needs to be immediate, Katniss sprints out for the table. Long before she makes it, a knife is launched at her, which she deftly avoids. She turns quickly and launches an arrow towards Clove, the knife-thrower, and only nicks her arm. Clove's next knife gets her right in the forehead, spilling blood into her eyes and causing her to stagger backwards. Clove follows the assault by tackling Katniss and pinning her to the ground.

Luckily for Katniss, Clove wants to relish her victory. She taunts Katniss rather than killing her immediately, mentioning how she and Cato want her dead, and taunting her with Rue's death. She is preparing to plunge the knife down when Thresh suddenly arrives and yanks her up. He has heard Clove's taunt about Rue, and in retaliation crushes her skull with a big stone. He confirms with Katniss that she was an ally of Rue's, and Katniss tells him about the bread. He decides to spare her life as restitution, and as they hear Cato calling out Clove's name and approaching, tells her to run.

Katniss grabs her gift and is gone to the woods, stopping to look back before she disappears into the brush. She sees Thresh has taken the rest of the presents and has disappeared into the field that appeared to be a steep cliff-drop. Katniss makes her way back to the cave, stopping to clean herself and the excess blood on the way, and then opens the package to find a hypodermic needle that she quickly uses to inject Peeta. After that, she passes out.

CHAPTER TWENTY-TWO

She wakes to the sound of rain, to find her head bandaged and Peeta's swelling diminished. Peeta has prepared food and rigged the cave to minimize leaks. As he feeds her, she tells him everything she's thus far kept secret, about Rue, the supplies, and finally about Thresh's gift. They talk a bit about what it means to owe a debt, and Katniss tells Peeta how much his bread gift meant so many years before. The pressures are starting to get to Katniss, and so Peeta encourages her to sleep more.

She wakes again that night, and they eat what little they have left. Peeta tells Katniss about the area Thresh is in – it's full of high grasses in which Thresh hid from the start of the Games. None of the Careers felt confident about trying to hunt him into such unpredictable territory. Katniss is led to compare Peeta, who is smart but safe, with Gale, who would likely not be deterred by a difficulty like this.

Because of their growing hunger, Katniss decides to ramp up the romance in hopes of attracting more gifts. She tries to open herself to him emotionally, and he responds by asking her not to die for him. His request makes her aware of how much she actually treasures him, and after a personal conversation, they share a warmer kiss than any they've shared thus far.

That night, they hold each other tight in the sleeping bag, and wake the next morning to find the weather is not improving. It is obviously Gamemaker designed, meant to starve them a bit. To continue tempting Haymitch to send gifts, Katniss asks more personal questions, which leads Peeta to share that he has loved her since he first saw her. It turns out that his father, the baker, was in love with Katniss's mother, but the latter ran off with her miner father because "even the birds [stopped] to listen" when he sang. Katniss is impressed with how well Peeta sells the romance angle, but for the first time grows suspicious about the "ring of truth" to his words, and whether that suggests true feelings behind what she assumes are otherwise lies for the camera. Their intimacy continues until she initiates a kiss, which is interrupted by a clang outside. They look out to find a parachute containing a veritable feast of food.

ANALYSIS

Though it is abundantly clear to the reader that Peeta's affection for Katniss is not feigned, she maintains her emotional distance by choosing to believe it's all motivated by playing to the spectacle. It is equally clear that her camaraderie with him is providing her great emotional support through the Games, but she almost completely refuses to acknowledge this. A trend is becoming apparent: Katniss, who long ago traded her childish innocence to protect her family, is best able to embrace her emotional side when she is taking care of someone. This is true of Rue and Prim and now of Peeta. Her insistence on not being in debt not only indicates her tendency to think in terms of functional stoic life, but also the discomfort it brings her to have to rely on others. The story of the goat also illustrates how she thrives on protecting others.

And yet, for a third time, it is her kindness and humanity that save her life. She is certainly dead at Clove's hand, until Thresh saves her and lets her live in restitution. Likewise, her affection towards Peeta earns them sponsor prizes, though she attributes this solely to the popularity of their love story. The long intimate conversation between Katniss and Peeta in Chapter 22 is full of dramatic irony, as the reader watches Katniss grow closer to Peeta while she convinces herself it's all a show. The metaphor of music-as-emotion surfaces in the conversation too, when Peeta's story about her and her father's singing were what drove others to fall for them.

The theme of identity is becoming more pronounced as she grows closer to Peeta. The closer she gets to him, the more she thinks of Gale and insists on comparing them. In some way, she is being forced to choose between two identities: a kind friend to the boy with the bread, or a tough-as-nails hunter.

Katniss is refusing to give in, and is still very aware of the audience, but her ethics are becoming more apparent. Thresh's kindness – seemingly selfless, and not to his advantage – confuses her, though we can see she is starting to understand, and she certainly can distinguish herself from Clove, who would have taken joy in dismembering her.

Summary and Analysis of Chapters 23-25

CHAPTER TWENTY-THREE

Katniss wisely forces them to eat in small portions, in case their malnutrition might force the rich food back up, wasting it. They chat more about Peeta's early infatuation, and Katniss daydreams a bit about what it would mean to be a winner, to live in the "Victor's Village" in a nice house provided by the Capitol. They make fun of Haymitch a bit, and Katniss wonders whether they are in fact more similar than she'd imagined.

The anthem plays, and Peeta sees in the sky that Thresh has died. Katniss is torn, between her pleasure at having one fewer tribute to face, and her disappointment over yet another death of someone she's come to have a relationship with. For the first time, she finds herself using the word "murder" in her thoughts.

Another effect of Thresh's death is that Cato will be on their tails again. So Peeta stays up on first watch, after which Katniss says a silent goodbye to Thresh before going to sleep. The next morning, they have some bread and Katniss learns that Peeta's family, though part of the merchant class as bakers, only eats the staler bread from their stores, a realization about class for Katniss.

The rain stops and Katniss takes stock of herself of her situation. She's been in the arena for what she assumes is two weeks, has seen the field narrow to four tributes, and she thinks about who she is below her hunter persona. The next morning, after a full breakfast and a show of romance for the cameras (again, she is impressed with Peeta's commitment to the illusion), they head out into the forest, and feel now back in the Games after their cave respite.

The storm has flooded the river. Peeta's lame leg makes him a loud companion, which makes hunting difficult. By the time they make it to Katniss's former hunting ground (around the area where she met Rue), Peeta sees through her euphemistic suggestions for quiet and demands to be told which roots to gather so that he won't sabotage her hunt. She does so, also teaching him a bird whistle.

Her hunting is successful and their whistle exchange keeps her confident he's okay. But when one of her whistles isn't returned, she rushes back to the spot to find some gathered berries in a pile, but no Peeta. When he arrives from gathering more roots, she breaks down a bit from her fear of having lost him, and notices someone has been eating some of the cheese (which was in the care package sent by Haymitch). They wonder who it could be when the cannon fires and then the hovercraft picks up a body nearby. They see Foxface lifted up to it, and Katniss pieces together that the berries he picked are poisonous and she must have eaten some.

CHAPTER TWENTY-FOUR

Despite the shock, they consider using the berries as a trap for Cato, and build a fire to see whether it draws him out. It does not. Peeta confesses he is a bit uncertain about sleeping in a tree, and isn't certain whether his leg can take the climb. Though they are several hours away from the cave, Katniss feels guilty about how she's treated Peeta for his noise, and so she acquiesces to his imprudent request to return.

By the time they get back, they are feeling the effects of being underfed and exhausted. But the heavy wind makes the cave seem like a smart place to be, and after he goes to sleep, Katniss kisses his forehead, "not for the audience, but for [her]." As she sits on watch, she reflects on Foxface's passing, admitting she admires the girl, and thinking about whether she can use Cato's temper against him. Peeta awakes near dawn and then she sleeps till the afternoon. They decide that, since the Gamemakers will likely soon be driving them all together, they will have a big meal to be ready.

They leave the cave later, knowing it will be for the last time. At this point, the rivers have been completely dried by the Gamemakers, meaning they'll have to head towards the lake. They head through the woods as Katniss reminisces on the horrors she's seen over the past few weeks. They make it to the plain but Cato is nowhere to be seen. They treat some water and rest, and Katniss whistles Rue's song, which then comes alive through the countryside via the mockingjays.

Suddenly, Cato comes smashing through the trees towards them. Katniss quickly launches an arrow, which bounces off his chest. They realize he has some type of body armor, but as he passes them, he only tosses them aside and continues running. It doesn't make sense, until Katniss looks towards the woods to see several creatures heading towards them.

CHAPTER TWENTY-FIVE

The creatures, obviously *muttations*, are wolf-men running on their hind legs. By instinct, Katniss takes off after Cato, who is heading towards the Cornucopia. It isn't until she's almost there that she remembers Peeta, and turns to see him limping about fifteen yards behind, with the creatures quickly catching up to him. There's nothing she can do, so she follows Cato again, this time climbing the Cornucopia and hoping the creatures can't climb.

As Cato tries to catch his breath and cease his cramping atop the structure, Katniss climbs part of the way and then shoots the muttations to keep them from climbing after Peeta. It's obvious their claws are prohibiting them from climbing after the humans, but one of them takes a running leap and lands on it. As it slides back down, Katniss makes a terrible realization: not only do the creature's eyes reveal it to be part human, but it's actually Glimmer, who's obviously been mutated by the

Gamemakers. She shoots it in the throat, a mercy kill. They realize that all of the creatures are the tribute corpses re-animated.

The creatures begin to leap along the sides, and one grabs Peeta's thigh in its teeth, almost dragging him off the Cornucopia. He uses his knife to free himself, but is soon after accosted by Cato, who paralyzes him in a headlock. Katniss has an arrow quickly ready, but it's a stand-off, since shooting Cato would undoubtedly cause Peeta to fall over as well. Using some of the blood from his wound, Peeta draws an "X" on Cato's hand, which Katniss correctly interprets as meaning that Cato's hands aren't shielded. She shoots an arrow into Cato's hand and causes him to fall over.

The body armor proves to be a liability, since it prolongs Cato's torture at the mercy of the creatures. He tries to fight his way out, but is ultimately dragged within the Cornucopia. That night, there's neither a cannon shot nor Cato's image in the sky, which means he's fading slowly under the creature's torture.

Meanwhile, Peeta's leg wound is intense, and the cold is progressively more severe. Katniss does her best with a tourniquet, using an arrow, and both just wait for Cato to die, hoping they don't perish first. By the next morning, they don't have much choice. Katniss leans precariously over the edge of the Cornucopia and, with her last arrow, shoots Cato from "pity, not vengeance." The cannon fires. Soon after, a hole opens in the plain and the creatures escape. However, no hovercraft appears until they move away from the structure in which Cato's body is now housed.

They wonder why nobody is ending the game when Claudius Templesmith's voice booms over the plain, announcing that the dual victor rule is no longer being honored. Peeta insists Katniss kill him, but she can't handle the idea. Suddenly, a stray comment of Peeta's about how the game has to have a victor gives her an idea. She realizes that audiences would revolt if their game had no victor, and perhaps the Gamemakers would be put to death by the Capitol. So she and Peeta both take a handful of the poisonous berries and prepare to eat them in a dual suicide. The gambit works, and Claudius Templesmith is suddenly yelling through the sky that they ought to stop, and he announces them both as the victors of the Seventy-fourth Hunger Games.

ANALYSIS

By the end of this section, Katniss's identity has been shaped, even if she's slow to being able to express it. First is her connection to Peeta. There is no question that her suicide ploy bears no functional value – that is, a pure stoic might not feel compelled to save his life. But their romance has grown and is full of genuine affection, even if she insists that it's all driven by the demands of the spectacle. This intimacy is aided by her continuing to see him more as a unique individual. She even gets the class realization that Peeta's family, while ostensibly middle class in District 12, still cannot eat their own fresh bread. The world is more complicated than she might have thought. The final class element in these chapters is the description of "Victor's

Village," a promise of wealth to the winning tribute. The social criticism in this is that the promise of wealth is yet another way that the people in charge keep the population in line.

This realization is even more manifest in her revolutionary zeal. She exhibits this in both private and public ways. In terms of the former, she silently mourns Thresh, understanding that they are linked both by a shared kindness and by their position as antagonists to the Capitol. For the first time, she uses the word "murder" to herself, acknowledging that the concept of a "game" is a construct that she will no longer subscribe to. Disgusted by the cruelty of reanimating dead tributes, she declares the Capitol her antagonist by refusing to play their game and potentially depriving them of a victor. Having learned that these acts of virtue and kindness yield dividends, she is not entirely taken aback when the ploy works and they are both named victors.

The mockingjay symbol reaches its fullest fruition in this section. When she hums Rue's melody as she and Peeta await Cato, she notes how beautifully it plays when repeated by the larger community of birds. This serves to illustrate that she is now thinking of herself in terms of her place in the world, not just in relation to herself. It is the awakening of a girl who might be a leader.

Lastly, she has firmly decided her identity in terms of values. She shoots Cato, who has been the most direct antagonist, explicitly out of pity and not vengeance. Katniss's ultimate success as a victor is due to having come to know herself and accept her contradictions. By balancing her stoic survival sense and empathy for others, she has attained a degree of self-knowledge that has proved significant in getting her to this point.

Summary and Analysis of Chapters 26-27

CHAPTER TWENTY-SIX

They both spit out the berries to the roar of the Capitol crowds, now being broadcast for them to hear. A hovercraft appears and Katniss grabs hold of Peeta so both are pulled up together. Peeta slumps from blood-loss almost right away, and doctors remove him, ready to operate. Katniss tries to stay with him, but is kept separated by a glass door. For the first time, she understands how it is her mother and Prim do not run away from a victim's wounds like she does: "it's because [they] have no choice" as healers. As Katniss stares into the glass, she sees her reflection and realizes how much she's suffered over the past weeks.

The hovercraft lands and they take Peeta away. Katniss tries to force herself in, but is knocked unconscious by needle. When she wakes, she is in a bed, in a room with no doors or windows. She's been cleaned, is comfortable, and she can hear from both ears! However, she cannot leave the bed, as she is belted into it, and she is attached to some fluids. After a while, the wall slides open and the redheaded Avox brings her dinner. Discreetly, she learns from the Avox that Peeta is alive. The food is simple broth, but she understands that they usually keep the tributes a few days before introducing them to the public so that the tributes can recover.

She weathers a few days of "continual twilight" as she recovers. Finally, she awakes one day to find she's no longer trapped in the bed. The wall slides open for her, and she walks through a hallway that boasts no doors, so she can't find Peeta quickly. She is looking around when she hears Effie's voice calling her name and then turns to see a chamber at the end of the hall, where wait Effie, Haymitch, and Cinna. She rushes down to them, no longer caring how she looks to the audiences, and convinced that they are merely keeping Peeta away so that the reunion can be televised. Meanwhile, Cinna is to prep her for her reintroduction to the public.

The prep team – Vinia, Flavius and Octavia – take care of her while she gets her first real meal. She notices how skinny she's gotten. While the team talks about the Games in a way that shows their disaffection from its real suffering, she forces herself to be tolerant. Cinna's designs for her are no longer fancy – instead, they include a simple dress with padding over her breasts to suggest more weight gained back. Overall, the effect is one of simplicity and female innocence. She doesn't understand the angle yet, but it does remind her that the Games aren't really done yet.

She meets her team in a chamber under the stage onto which she will soon be raised for her reunion with Peeta. Haymitch strangely asks her for a hug, and while in the embrace, whispers to her that she's in trouble – the Capitol's furious for her threat to stage a suicide, and wants revenge. Her only defense, he tells her, will be to really sell the lovers angle, since the spectacle of a love-crazed girl would make it seem less an act of rebellion. She asks if he's told Peeta the plan, and Haymitch answers cryptically, "Don't have to...He's already there."

She is in a great state of confusion, about what her rebellion meant, about how she feels about Peeta, about how she can manage this potentially dangerous situation, when the platform raises her to the stage.

CHAPTER TWENTY-SEVEN

The crowd goes wild as she is raised up, and she suddenly understands that Cinna's simple design is meant to further the image Haymitch needs her to present. She looks over to Peeta, cleaned and handsome, and throws herself into his arms, where he kisses her as the crowd goes wild again.

They sit together on a small couch, and Katniss leans into him intimately. Caesar Flickman, the host again, introduces the program (which is mandatory viewing for all citizens) and then they watch a re-cap video. Katniss realizes it's been edited to emphasize the love story. She notices how well Peeta "sells" the love story angle, even before they reunited in the arena, whereas she seems callous and self-interested for her survival techniques. She hates watching the death of other tributes, and is moved to see her goodbye to Rue replayed. They do not show the image of Rue's corpse decorated with flowers – "even that smacks of rebellion." The video follows them up through her banging on the glass door in the hovercraft wanting be closer to Peeta during his surgery.

After the video, President Snow brings out a crown that splits into two. Despite his apparent joy, Katniss sees his unforgiving eyes up close. After the show, they are brought to the President's house for a Victory Banquet, where they are the center of attention, mainly taking pictures with sponsors and important people.

When they get back, they are quickly separated and led to their rooms. Katniss wants to try and find Peeta to talk, but her bedroom door is locked. The next morning, she is awoken and reminded she needs to get ready for her interview. After a quick breakfast, Cinna dresses her, again emphasizing simplicity, and she meets Caesar for an interview, this time just in front of cameras and not a live audience. Peeta comes out to meet her, and reminds her in secret that Haymitch won't be able to keep them apart once they're back home. The comment makes her feel guilty, but she doesn't have time to analyze the feelings.

Again, she curls up next to him to push the image. Peeta handles most of the difficult questions with his characteristic charm, but Caesar finally asks her when she fell in love with Peeta. She has no answer, but he offers maybe it was when she called his name out after the dual victor announcement (see Chapter 18). Through the conversation, Katniss learns that Peeta lost his leg in the surgery and now has a fake limb. She feels guilty, as though her poor tourniquet was the problem. Overall, they perform extremely well in selling the defense that, regarding the berries move, Katniss was madly in love.

Back in her room, Katniss finds the mockingjay pin has been returned to her. She and Peeta take a car to a train that will take them home for a few months before they are to tour the districts. Finally, the train leaves the station and Katniss begins to feel free again. After a huge dinner, she changes her clothes and make-up and forces herself to remember who she is – a hunter who "lives in the Seam."

The train makes a brief stop, and Katniss finds herself thinking of Gale. She and Peeta walk a bit away, but Haymitch catches them and congratulates them on pulling off the strategy. Peeta is confused but quickly realizes that Katniss's affection for him was all "for the Games." She insists it wasn't all that way, but "the closer we get to District Twelve, the more confused I get." Nevertheless, Peeta is crushed and walks away.

She grapples with herself about how to express her confusion, to explain that she already misses him. But there isn't much time to reach any decision before they arrive back at their district. Peeta holds out his hand, ready to sell the picture one last time. Katniss isn't ready to declare herself one way or the other, but the door is about to open. She gets ready to confront this next, very different, section of the Hunger Games.

ANALYSIS

Katniss's understanding of the Capitol (and its spectacle) as antagonist gains a lot of traction in this final section. The reader realizes (and Katniss sees up close) that the spectacle really isn't the fight to the death but is much larger. Her self-awareness and firm identity proved benefits in the ring, but in this next phase they will prove fatal liability. So she has to continue crafting herself an image, and continue to play to the spectacle. But unlike the beginning of her adventure, now she knows who her enemy is, and while she doesn't make any explicit statement of intent, the reader can guess that Katniss is not through fighting.

In fact, she seems to have gained great insight into how these Games separate people from one another. Her feelings about the prep team when they blather on about the Games in a detached manner are disgusting to her, but she understands that they are not actually enemies – instead, they are equal victims of the mind control engendered by this spectacle. Katniss has seen through it, though, suggesting a conflict yet to come. Before she leaves the Capitol, Cinna makes sure she has her mockingjay pin, also indicating that the revolution is just beginning.

The obvious and horrific injustices aside, the spectacle also confuses her about her identity. Certainly, she curls up to Peeta and plays the lovers angle out of self-preservation, but she also gains comfort from it. The irony is she would love to explore these feelings with Peeta, but she's forced to be so close to him in a proscribed way that only confuses more.

Her identity is further confused by class differences. As they approach the Seam, she transforms herself back to the girl she believes she is. However much she's grown and changed over the previous few weeks, she wants to treat this new identity as though it was merely constructed for the Games. She is unable to tell Peeta how deeply she cares. She is "the girl from the Seam" and they don't run in the same circles.

The novel suitably ends with these conflicts still simmering, since this is the first volume of a trilogy. Katniss has in her a revolutionary spark and a great insight that sees the truth of their unjust world head-on, but she's still a very young woman, and has much more to learn about herself than she ever thought.

Suggested Essay Questions

1.

In what ways is all of Panem complicit in the horrors of the Hunger Games?

Though the Capitol most actively runs the Games, it could be argued that the entire society grants its support by refusing to boycott or challenge the ubiquitous Games. Katniss does note that law requires citizens to follow the Games, but throughout the book are indications of the population's wild support. When Katniss volunteers to take Prim's place, her district shows its dissent against the Games by refusing to applaud, which suggests that refusal to honor the Games is an option, even if it might carry punishment. Though capable of rebellion (they did revolt once before), the population of Panem lacks the strength to question and challenge their system, instead allowing themselves to be led through spectacle.

2.

Discuss the ways in which Katniss's poverty has shaped her.

Katniss's poverty proves both useful and debilitating to her. Because of her lack of privilege, she has been forced to learn several skills that prove useful in the arena. In addition to her hunting and gathering aptitude, she comments several times on how she knows how to scrounge and her body is able to manage hunger better than those accustomed to luxury. However, her class resentments blind her a bit to certain other assets. Most tellingly, this happens with Peeta, who she considers "soft" and inferior to Gale even after Peeta begins to show his fortitude.

3.

Contrast what Gale and Peeta signify for Katniss, and how each helps her succeed in the Games.

For Katniss, Gale is a symbol of the toughness engendered by poverty, where Peeta is a symbol of selfless kindness. Much of the novel is her learning to accept that both elements are a part of her character. Gale's influence proves extremely useful in the arena, as Katniss uses her stoic demeanor and hunting aptitude to stay alive. However, her ultimate victory comes for being able to trust others, a virtue she first learned when Peeta gave her bread years before. Even in the arena, Peeta's kindness continues to affect Katniss, until she ultimately refuses to win the contest unless they win together.

4. **Trace Katniss's growth from determined stoic to a fuller human being, using examples to illustrate each phrase of her character growth.**

At the beginning of the novel, Katniss is a committed stoic, who keeps her features in an "indifferent mask" to aid her survival through tough conditions. After being named tribute but before going to the arena, she is confronted both with her guilt at not helping the Avox, and with Peeta's "purity" of wanting to stay himself until death despite the barbaric pressures of the arena. Peeta's seeming betrayal convinces her a stoic philosophy is best, but she nevertheless allies with Rue and comes to accept her emotional side when she plans Rue's funeral. This happens in larger scale when she decides to help nurse Peeta back to health, and falls for him despite herself. Finally, she refuses to win the Games unless they win together, even if the cost is suicide. By the end of the novel, Katniss is far more confused than at the beginning, but this confusion indicates that she is becoming a much fuller person.

5. **Discuss the influences of ancient civilizations on The Hunger Games.**

The influence of both Greek and Roman civilizations is significant in the novel. The Greek influence starts with the story of Theseus and the Minotaur, which is a similar tale of children forced to fight to their deaths, a strategy used by the ruler to keep the population in line. The idea of the Roman games, brutal events that gave the lower classes a spectacle to discourage rebellion, is also central to the conception of the Hunger Games. Several of the names in the novel help further this connection, as does the idea of tesserae.

6. **Explain the various methods used by the Capitol to keep its population in line. How does the Capitol keep citizens from connecting with one another, and why are these strategies successful?**

The most obvious strategy is the spectacle of the Hunger Games. By distracting its population from the true injustices of Panem, the Capitol keeps them from considering rebellion. This strategy is successful in no small part because it makes the population somewhat complicit in the brutality. Class divisions are another way the Capitol discourages dissent. By separating the Districts from one another along strict lines of wealth, and then encouraging class resentment through tesserae, the Capitol keeps citizens distrustful of one another so that they will not turn their eyes collectively towards their true oppressor. Lastly, the Capitol keeps the Districts from knowing much about one another. Katniss learns this when she talks with Rue about District 11, and notes to the reader that the Capitol is probably not airing their conversation in order to discourage education.

7.

What do you think is the reasoning behind Haymitch's unified front stategy for Peeta and Katniss? What are the effects of the strategy, and why does it work?

The most direct aim of Haymitch's strategy is to create a narrative in the Games that will attract sponsors and hence help Katniss and Peeta in the arena. Haymitch likely gets the idea when he realizes Peeta is in love with Katniss, and knows that their "love story" will make them popular. But the effects of the strategy are more wide-reaching. Katniss, so conflicted by her commitment to stoicism and her class resentments, might have had more trouble trusting Peeta if she hadn't had the excuse that it was all part of the show. By using this defense, she is able to delude herself that she isn't actually falling for Peeta, even though it's clear to the reader that she has feelings for him. Finally, the strategy has a touch of rebellion to it. The whole concept of the Hunger Games is to keep people separate from one another, to discourage rebellion. But this plan actually suggests community, and that manifests in Katniss's suicide ploy at the end of the Games. She uses the love narrative to protect herself once they return to the world, but the rebellious sense of community has already been suggested.

8.

How does the first-person narration help establish the themes of the novel?

Most of the story's themes involve Katniss's growth as a person. The theme of identity and the contradictions Katniss feels are aided by the irony that exists between what she observes in herself and what the reader observes. It is clear to the reader that Katniss is slowly learning to accept her emotional side as a strength, but because she is narrating the story in present tense, she isn't always able to recognize that in herself. This is most clear in her relationship with Peeta, where she insists that her affection is mostly for the show, even as her feelings are clearly genuine. The theme of rebellion also manifests even as the narrator does not recognize it. She learns to accept community as a source of strength throughout the novel, though her primary stated goal remains survival. Because Katniss is our only lens to the story, it explores how our identity is shaped even when we don't recognize it.

9.

Suzanne Collins has stated that reality television, which offers usually the appearance of reality rather than reality itself, is one of her influences in the novel. How is that influence manifested in Panem?

The Hunger Games is meant to offer Panem a brutally realistic glimpse into human nature and adventure. However, the entire event is in truth about superficial image rather than reality. This is clear from the first stages, in which the tributes are introduced to the audiences through high-profile events. The amount of work that goes into shaping their images suggests that what the audience sees are not the tributes themselves, but rather a shaped image of them. Katniss goes through much preparation with her prep team and Cinna, and she and Peeta stay near each other not from any true feeling, but because Haymitch has told them to. And then in the Games themselves, the Gamemakers frequently change the rules and the environment in order to up the entertainment value. Overall, the appearance of reality is all that matters in the Hunger Games.

10.

Discuss the use of fire in the novel, and what it tells us about the protagonist.

Katniss's story is one of adolescent growth, as she learns to accept her passionate side as a strength, and additionally to translate that into a revolutionary zeal. Fire is traditionally an image of strong passion. But the irony is that when Cinna establishes her as "the girl who was on fire," she doesn't yet realize what he sees in her. Through the novel, she learns to rely on this part of herself, which is reflecting in her desire to keep her fingernails painted. By the end, she no longer needs the spectacle of fire to accept her firey personality. Fire is also the key to survival and strategy throughout – lighting fires is how she tries to distract the Careers in several cases, and the Gamemakers use fire at one point to attack her. All of this suggests that strength for Katniss will come first from accepting her passionate side, and then afterwards learning to control her passions to become a powerful figure.

The story of Theseus and the Minotaur

In several interviews, Suzanne Collins cites the Greek myth of Theseus and the Minotaur as a significant influence on the world of Panem. It is worth considering the story since the similarities and differences can prove illuminating.

As related by Edith Hamilton in her classic volume *Mythology*, the story is one of a hero rescuing an oppressed society from brutal strictures. Minos, the king of Crete, once sent his only son on a visit to Athens, and the boy was sent by the Athenian king to fight a dangerous bull. When the boy died on the expedition, the angry Minos captured Athens and declared that he would destroy it unless they acquiesced to his bizarre demand: once every nine years, the Athenians had to send a tribute of seven maidens and seven youths, who would then be forced to confront the Minotaur, who would devour them.

The Minotaur was a hall-bull and half-human creature. Minos had trapped the creature in a specially constructed labyrinth, and he would cruelly put the 14 Athenian tributes into the labyrinth so that they were not only killed by the creature, but forced to attempt escape from an inevitable end, thus prolonging their agony.

Theseus, a Greek hero with a great destiny, arrived in Athens one year shortly before the tributes were due, and he volunteered to serve as a male tribute. The citizens were touched by his bravery, not knowing he also intended to slay the beast. When removed to Crete and paraded before the citizens there, he caught the eye of Minos's daughter, who fell in love with him and offered him a boon towards survival – she gave him a ball of yarn that he could unravel as he explored the labyrinth, so that should he kill the creature, he could find his way out. He succeeded both in killing the creature and escaping, and ultimately was named King of Athens after other adventures.

This story resonates in several ways with *The Hunger Games*. Though the citizens of Athens were suitably horrified by their plight (whereas Panem is distracted by the spectacle of the television program), Katniss has an awareness of injustice and a stoic strength that recalls Theseus. Likewise, she succeeds not only through her personal strength, but through love, in her case with Peeta, in Theseus's case with Minos's daughter. Lastly, the unnecessary cruelty involved with both games – the arena is, after all, just another type of unbeatable labyrinth – suggests the depths of evil that humans can reach, even when separated by thousands of years. It is key to themes of the trilogy that the brutality of Panem's regime is not unique. Victorious powers have long demanded tributes from their conquests that crippled the conquered people and, sometimes, these tributes were in the form of people. Although historically human tributes were more likely kept alive as slaves rather than fed to angry hybrids, the Greek myth shows that such brutality has long been part of the human imagination.

Author of ClassicNote and Sources

S.R. Cedars, author of ClassicNote. Completed on October 16, 2011, copyright held by GradeSaver.

Updated and revised Elizabeth Weinbloom December 06, 2012. Copyright held by GradeSaver.

Sarah Rees Brennan, Jennifer Lynn Barnes, et al. Ed. Leah Wilson. The Girl Who Was On Fire: Your Favorite Authors on Suzanne Collins' Hunger Games Trilogy. Dallas, TX: BellaBooks, 2010.

Edith Hamilton. Mythology. New York: Signet Classics, 1969.

School Library Journal. "A Killer Story: An Interview with Suzanne Collins, Author of 'The Hunger Games'." 2011-10-15. <http://www.schoollibraryjournal.com/article/CA6590063.html>.

"The Games." 2011-10-15. <http://www.roman-empire.net/society/soc-games.html>.

Stanford Encyclopedia of Philosophy. "Stoicism." 2011-10-15. <http://plato.stanford.edu/entries/stoicism/>.

Quiz 1

1. **What is the name of the ceremony where tributes are chosen from each district?**
   A. The Treaty of Treason
   B. The Seam
   C. The Hunger Games
   D. The Reaping

2. **What district is Katniss from?**
   A. District 2
   B. District 4
   C. District 11
   D. District 12

3. **What is the name of the area where Katniss lives?**
   A. The Seam
   B. The Meadow
   C. The Armpit
   D. The Hob

4. **What is the weapon with which Katniss is most proficient?**
   A. Bow
   B. Hand-to-hand
   C. Knife
   D. Sword

5. **What is the primary occupation of Katniss's district?**
   A. Bakers
   B. Electronic Engineers
   C. Agricultural Workers
   D. Coal Miners

6. **What is Katniss's mother's profession?**
   A. Hunter
   B. Miner
   C. Dancer
   D. Healer

7. **What does Peeta's family do for a living?**
    A. Bakers
    B. Miners
    C. Hunters
    D. Agricultural Workers

8. **Why was Katniss given a medal by her district's mayor when she was young?**
    A. Her hunting ability
    B. Her victory of the Hunger Games
    C. Her father's death
    D. Her stoicism

9. **What is the name of the system through which poor people can buy food through additional Hunger Game entries?**
    A. Trading
    B. Tesserae
    C. Tributes
    D. The Reaping

10. **What happened to the thirteenth colony?**
    A. It moved to "Victory Village"
    B. It won the Hunger Games
    C. It was destroyed
    D. It was never built

11. **What is the trading post of Katniss's district called?**
    A. The Seam
    B. The Meadow
    C. The Reaping
    D. The Hob

12. **What age does a child first have to enter the Hunger Games lottery?**
    A. 12
    B. 14
    C. 16
    D. 18

13. **What does the audience do after Katniss volunteers to take Prim's place as tribute?**
    A. They cry
    B. A supportive gesture
    C. They rebel
    D. They applaud

14. **Who gives Katniss the mockingjay pin?**
    A. Her mother
    B. Gale
    C. Prim
    D. Madge

15. **Who does not visit Katniss in the Justice Center?**
    A. Peeta's Father
    B. Gale
    C. Prim
    D. Peeta

16. **Where is Katniss's district located (in terms of the faded North American continent)?**
    A. Florida
    B. The South
    C. Appalachia
    D. The Rockies

17. **What is the name of Katniss and Peeta's district representative from the Capitol?**
    A. Peeta Mellark
    B. Effie Trinket
    C. Mayor Undersee
    D. Haymitch Abernathy

18. **Who is not a member of Katniss's prep team?**
    A. Octavia
    B. Flavius
    C. Haymitch
    D. Cinna

19. **What is the name of Katniss's stylist?**
    A. Portia
    B. Octavia
    C. Flavius
    D. Cinna

20. **What is the name of Peeta's stylist?**
    A. Portia
    B. Octavia
    C. Flavius
    D. Cinna

21. **What is an Avox?**
    A. A Hunger Games victor
    B. A servant
    C. A district representative to the Games
    D. A punished criminal

22. **What does Peeta say his most useful skill for the arena will be?**
    A. Archery
    B. Knife Throwing
    C. Camouflage
    D. Hand-to-hand

23. **How are the Gamemakers dressed?**
    A. Hunger Games outfits
    B. Business Suits
    C. Non-descript clothing
    D. Purple Robes

24. **Who is the Capitol representative who runs the Training Center?**
    A. Effie Trinket
    B. Haymitch
    C. Atala
    D. Cinna

25. **During the training, who does Peeta say is their "shadow?"**
   A. Glimmer
   B. Rue
   C. Cato
   D. Clove

Quiz 1 Answer Key

1. **(D)** The Reaping
2. **(D)** District 12
3. **(A)** The Seam
4. **(A)** Bow
5. **(D)** Coal Miners
6. **(D)** Healer
7. **(A)** Bakers
8. **(C)** Her father's death
9. **(B)** Tesserae
10. **(C)** It was destroyed
11. **(D)** The Hob
12. **(A)** 12
13. **(B)** A supportive gesture
14. **(D)** Madge
15. **(D)** Peeta
16. **(C)** Appalachia
17. **(B)** Effie Trinket
18. **(C)** Haymitch
19. **(D)** Cinna
20. **(A)** Portia
21. **(D)** A punished criminal
22. **(C)** Camouflage
23. **(D)** Purple Robes
24. **(C)** Atala
25. **(B)** Rue

Quiz 2

1. **What does Katniss call the tributes who train in anticipation of the Games?**
   A. Careers
   B. Cheaters
   C. Sponsors
   D. Fools

2. **Which station does Katniss visit during the Training Sessions?**
   A. Archery
   B. Weight Lifting
   C. Knot Tying
   D. Hand-to-hand

3. **What are the Gamemakers eating when Katniss is called to her individual session?**
   A. Lamb Stew
   B. Roasted Pig
   C. A groosling
   D. A muttation

4. **What score do the Gamemakers give to Katniss?**
   A. 2
   B. 7
   C. 8
   D. 11

5. **What score do the Gamemakers give to Peeta?**
   A. 2
   B. 6
   C. 8
   D. 11

6. **What does Gale call Katniss?**
   A. Catnip
   B. Katniss
   C. Lover Girl
   D. Sweetheart

7. **Who is the interview host for the pre-Games interviews?**
   A. Effie Trinket
   B. Claudius Templesmith
   C. Caesar Flickerman
   D. Haymitch Abernathy

8. **What is Katniss's favorite food in the Capitol?**
   A. The pie
   B. Lamb Stew
   C. The fruit
   D. Creme Brulee

9. **Who is the ruler of Panem?**
   A. President Abernathy
   B. Madame Trinket
   C. Kaiser Mellark
   D. President Snow

10. **What does Haymitch identify as Katniss's most difficult quality that she must overcome to do well in the interview?**
    A. Her Hostility
    B. Her Beauty
    C. Her Intelligence
    D. Her Sadness

11. **What uncharacteristic move does Katniss use during the pre-Games interview?**
    A. She spits in the interviewer's face
    B. She twirls and giggles
    C. She stays silent
    D. She dances

12. **What does Peeta confess in the pre-Games interview?**
    A. He wants to train apart from Katniss
    B. He hates Katniss
    C. He has a crush on Katniss
    D. He expects to win

13. **What does Katniss do to Peeta after the pre-Games interview?**
   A. Kisses Him
   B. Shoves Him
   C. Ignores Him
   D. Makes him cry

14. **What does Haymitch advise should be their first action in the Games?**
   A. Attack the nearby tributes
   B. Find each other
   C. Find water
   D. Collect supplies

15. **What does Cinna do with Katniss's fingernails?**
   A. Paint them
   B. Ignore Them
   C. Arm Them as Weapons
   D. Take Them Off

16. **What is the one de facto rule of the arena?**
   A. No cannibalism
   B. No making fires
   C. No killing
   D. No posing for the TV

17. **How does the Capitol follow Katniss in the arena?**
   A. She checks in to posts
   B. A tracker implanted in her arm
   C. Hidden Representatives
   D. Hovercrafts

18. **Who is the Capitol announcer for the games?**
   A. President Snow
   B. Claudius Templesmith
   C. Caeser Flickerman
   D. Haymitch Abernathy

19. **Katniss is participating in what year of the Hunger Games?**
    A. 10th
    B. 74th
    C. 100th
    D. 124th

20. **What happens to tributes if they step off their metal circle before the gong is sounded?**
    A. Nothing
    B. They are forced to start again
    C. They drown
    D. They explode

21. **What is the structure containing supplies (in the arena) called?**
    A. The Lake
    B. The Reaping
    C. Cornucopia
    D. The Bloodbath

22. **What does Katniss call the initial rush for supplies once the gong is sounded?**
    A. The Seam
    B. The Supplies Rush
    C. The Opening
    D. The Bloodbath

23. **What does Katniss fetch after the gong is sounded?**
    A. A backpack
    B. A bow
    C. Infection Medicine
    D. A knife

24. **Why doesn't Katniss rush for more supplies when the gong is sounded?**
    A. She trips
    B. She is attacked by Clove
    C. She wishes to follow Haymitch's advice
    D. She is distracted by Peeta

25. **Which tribute is proficient with knives?**

A. Foxface
B. Glimmer
C. Cato
D. Clove

Quiz 2 Answer Key

1. (**A**) Careers
2. (**C**) Knot Tying
3. (**B**) Roasted Pig
4. (**D**) 11
5. (**C**) 8
6. (**A**) Catnip
7. (**C**) Caesar Flickerman
8. (**B**) Lamb Stew
9. (**D**) President Snow
10. (**A**) Her Hostility
11. (**B**) She twirls and giggles
12. (**C**) He has a crush on Katniss
13. (**B**) Shoves Him
14. (**C**) Find water
15. (**A**) Paint them
16. (**A**) No cannibalism
17. (**B**) A tracker implanted in her arm
18. (**B**) Claudius Templesmith
19. (**B**) 74th
20. (**D**) They explode
21. (**C**) Cornucopia
22. (**D**) The Bloodbath
23. (**A**) A backpack
24. (**D**) She is distracted by Peeta
25. (**D**) Clove

Quiz 3

1. **What signifies the death of a tribute in the arena?**
   A. Cannon
   B. Images in the sky
   C. Claudius Templesmith's announcement
   D. Anthem Plays

2. **Where does Katniss sleep in the first nights of the Games?**
   A. In a bush
   B. Treetops
   C. A cave
   D. By the water supply

3. **How can tributes follow which other tributes died in the Games?**
   A. Images in the sky
   B. Claudius Templesmith's announcement
   C. Silver Parachutes
   D. Anthem Plays

4. **How are sponsor gifts sent to tributes?**
   A. By Cornucopia
   B. By Silver parachutes
   C. By tracker jackers
   D. By messenger

5. **Why is iodine important to Katniss?**
   A. To treat water
   B. To clean wounds
   C. To blow up enemies
   D. To stay warm

6. **Who sends the "wall of fire" at Katniss?**
   A. Careers
   B. Haymitch
   C. Rue
   D. Gamemakers

7. **What are the Capitol-mutated wasps called?**
    A. Tracker Jackers
    B. Jabberjays
    C. Mockingjays
    D. Cornucopias

8. **Who warns Katniss about the presence of the tracker jacker nest?**
    A. Haymitch
    B. Rue
    C. Cato
    D. Peeta

9. **What does Katniss get from Glimmer after she is attacked by wasps?**
    A. Bow
    B. Food
    C. Infection Medicine
    D. Sword

10. **Who is not stung by wasps?**
    A. Katniss
    B. Rue
    C. Cato
    D. Peeta

11. **Why is Katniss uncertain whether Peeta actually saves her life or not following the wasp incident?**
    A. Iodine
    B. Sadness
    C. Deafness
    D. Hallucinations

12. **What district is Rue from?**
    A. District 2
    B. District 4
    C. District 11
    D. District 12

13. **What is Rue's district's primary industry?**
   A. Banking
   B. Coal Mining
   C. Electronics
   D. Agriculture

14. **What item from Katniss's supplies does Rue explain to her?**
   A. Iodine
   B. Arrows
   C. Sunglasses
   D. Silver Parachutes

15. **What is Rue's great passion?**
   A. Cooking
   B. Medicine
   C. Friendship
   D. Music

16. **What does Katniss overhear Cato say he did to Peeta?**
   A. He forgave him
   B. He betrayed him
   C. He cut him
   D. He killed him

17. **Why is the small boy from District 3 part of the Career path?**
   A. He engineered landmines
   B. He is a good fighter
   C. He is connected to the Gamemakers
   D. He knows how to swim

18. **What does Katniss use to set off the landmines?**
   A. Apples
   B. Bushes
   C. Foxface
   D. Bombs

19. **What is the most lasting injury Katniss suffers from the mine explosion?**
    A. Deafness
    B. Broken Arm
    C. Kills Peeta
    D. Loses Her Bow

20. **Who else is happy to see the Careers supplies destroyed?**
    A. Foxface
    B. Glimmer
    C. Cato
    D. Clove

21. **Who kills Rue?**
    A. Thresh
    B. An unnamed boy
    C. Cato
    D. Clove

22. **What does Katniss not do after Rue dies?**
    A. Bury Rue
    B. Sing to Rue
    C. Grow angry at the Capitol
    D. Decorate Rue's body with flowers

23. **What is Katniss's first gift from sponsors?**
    A. Burn Ointment
    B. Infection Medicine
    C. A pot of broth
    D. A feast

24. **What does Katniss receive after Rue's death as a sponsor gift?**
    A. A loaf of bread
    B. Burn Ointment
    C. Infection Medicine
    D. A pot of broth

25. **What does Katniss do immediately after the Gamemakers change the victor rules?**
    A. Bury Rue
    B. Cry
    C. Go to sleep
    D. Scream Peeta's name

Quiz 3 Answer Key

1. **(A)** Cannon
2. **(B)** Treetops
3. **(A)** Images in the sky
4. **(B)** By Silver parachutes
5. **(A)** To treat water
6. **(D)** Gamemakers
7. **(A)** Tracker Jackers
8. **(B)** Rue
9. **(A)** Bow
10. **(B)** Rue
11. **(D)** Hallucinations
12. **(C)** District 11
13. **(D)** Agriculture
14. **(C)** Sunglasses
15. **(D)** Music
16. **(C)** He cut him
17. **(A)** He engineered landmines
18. **(A)** Apples
19. **(A)** Deafness
20. **(A)** Foxface
21. **(B)** An unnamed boy
22. **(A)** Bury Rue
23. **(A)** Burn Ointment
24. **(A)** A loaf of bread
25. **(D)** Scream Peeta's name

Quiz 4

1. **Where does Katniss find Peeta?**
    A. Hiding in a cave
    B. Hiding in a river
    C. Living with the Careers
    D. Living with Thresh

2. **Katniss believes Haymitch sends her a message with his gifts: "one kiss equals one ____."**
    A. Life Saved
    B. Packet of Medicine
    C. Pot of broth
    D. Piece of food

3. **What story does Katniss tell Peeta when he wants a story to calm him?**
    A. The story of District 13
    B. The story of Gale
    C. The story of Lady the Goat
    D. The story of the Treaty of Treason

4. **Where do Katniss and Peeta set up camp to recover?**
    A. In a cave
    B. By the lake
    C. In the trees
    D. By the river

5. **How does Katniss get away from Peeta to attend the "feast?"**
    A. Kisses
    B. Lies
    C. Sleep syrup
    D. The story of the Treaty of Treason

6. **Who claims the first gift from the "feast"?**
    A. Foxface
    B. Glimmer
    C. Katniss
    D. Clove

7. **Who kills Clove?**
   A. Thresh
   B. Foxface
   C. Katniss
   D. Peeta

8. **What is Katniss's gift from the "feast"?**
   A. Burn Ointment
   B. Body Armor
   C. Books
   D. Infection Medicine

9. **Why does Peeta's father say Katniss's mother married her father?**
   A. His anger
   B. His singing voice
   C. His sense of humor
   D. His mining ability

10. **How does Foxface die?**
   A. Katniss
   B. Landmines
   C. She drowns
   D. Poisonous Berries

11. **Who chases Cato to the final confrontation?**
   A. The Gamemakers
   B. Katniss
   C. Muttations
   D. Peeta

12. **What does the Capitol do with the corpses of the dead tributes?**
   A. Reanimate them
   B. Hide them
   C. Burn them
   D. Bury them

13. **Who kills Cato?**
    A. The Gamemakers
    B. Katniss
    C. The muttations
    D. Peeta

14. **Where do the creatures go after Cato dies?**
    A. Into a hole in the ground
    B. Into a cave
    C. Into the lake
    D. Onto the Cornucopia

15. **What does Katniss propose when the Gamemakers rescind their rule change?**
    A. She kill Peeta
    B. A dual suicide
    C. Peeta kill her
    D. They run away

16. **How does Cinna dress Katniss for her reintroduction to the public?**
    A. A simple dress
    B. He paints her body
    C. A fancy gown
    D. He lights her on fire

17. **What strange request does Haymitch make before Katniss is reintroduced to the public?**
    A. Slap the Interviewer
    B. Ignore Him
    C. Ignore Peeta
    D. Give him a hug

18. **In whose eyes does Katniss see anger at the post-show interview?**
    A. President Snow
    B. Claudius Templesmith
    C. Caeser Flickerman
    D. An audience member

19. **What surgery does Peeta have to have after the Games?**
    A. Leg amputation
    B. Plastic Surgery
    C. Open heart surgery
    D. Muscle Enhancement

20. **Where do Peeta and Katniss go after the Games are over?**
    A. To live with President Snow
    B. To tour the districts
    C. Back home
    D. To District 13

21. **How many Hunger Games victors has Katniss's district provided before she wins?**
    A. 0
    B. 1
    C. 2
    D. 12

22. **Where do the Hunger Games victors get to live?**
    A. The Seam
    B. Victor's Village
    C. District 13
    D. The Capitol

23. **Where does Peeta realize that Katniss might have been faking her affection for him?**
    A. As a stop on the train journey
    B. In the interview
    C. In the arena
    D. On the train

24. **Why is the Capitol upset with Katniss after the Games?**
    A. For being a girl victor
    B. For her rebellious act
    C. For loving Peeta
    D. For declaring them evil

25. **How does Katniss feel on her train ride from the Captitol after the Games?**

   A. Feisty
   B. Confused
   C. Happy
   D. In Love

Quiz 4 Answer Key

1. **(B)** Hiding in a river
2. **(C)** Pot of broth
3. **(C)** The story of Lady the Goat
4. **(A)** In a cave
5. **(C)** Sleep syrup
6. **(A)** Foxface
7. **(A)** Thresh
8. **(D)** Infection Medicine
9. **(B)** His singing voice
10. **(D)** Poisonous Berries
11. **(C)** Muttations
12. **(A)** Reanimate them
13. **(B)** Katniss
14. **(A)** Into a hole in the ground
15. **(B)** A dual suicide
16. **(A)** A simple dress
17. **(D)** Give him a hug
18. **(A)** President Snow
19. **(A)** Leg amputation
20. **(C)** Back home
21. **(C)** 2
22. **(B)** Victor's Village
23. **(A)** As a stop on the train journey
24. **(B)** For her rebellious act
25. **(B)** Confused

Made in the USA
Lexington, KY
06 February 2012